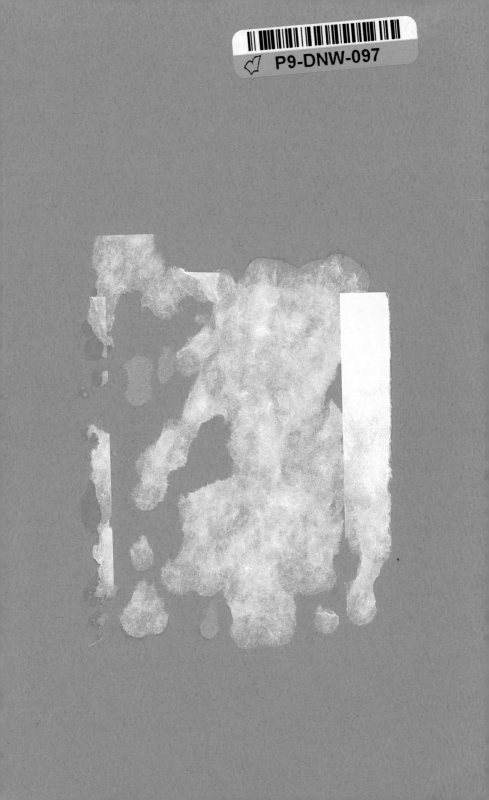

Talking to Myself

Also by Pearl Bailey
The Raw Pearl

Pearl Bailey

New York

Talking to Myself

Harcourt Brace Jovanovich, Inc.

Dedicated
To Humanity
In Love
Pearl

Introduction

The idea of writing another book came to me while I was in *Hello, Dolly!* The fantastic success of that whole experience inspired me. People were leaving their seats to run up to the stage. That's how wild it was. The people in the audience were forgetting themselves. People who would never dream of moving from their seats except to leave the theater or to go to the rest room would come to the runway to shake hands with me. And many of them would be shouting, "God bless you, God bless you, God bless you." I would tell them, "He does, continuously, He does."

I don't think that people can possibly know what an emotional charge that is for me. It is rich and filling sustenance for times when I'm tired, with my bones aching, overcome by mental and physical fatigue. The memory helps me recover, charge up again, and go out to the stage. I go not just to hear that thunderous applause. I go to experience "that thing," whatever it was or is. So much larger than the audience or me or all of us together. Dedication is a gift of God.

Sometimes I had to drop out of the show. Sheer exhaustion. Doctors' warning of possible death. Yet (and this amazes me too), no pain and no threat could make me stay away for very long. I often returned to the stage more tired physically than when I left, but mentally rested. Many of the pros and veterans of the theater have told me that they have seen nothing to equal the event that occurred between the people onstage and the people in the audience at a typical performance of *Hello, Dolly!* All of us in the business have seen ovations, the stupendous kind. Usually they happen when the house is packed with friends and relatives, "a papered house." I am here to tell you that when it happens spontaneously, in a genuine way, from the heart, it is a different thing all together. I saw it happen from the last row of the top balcony to the front row of the orchestra, every night and every matinee. I could feel the warmth of people I couldn't even see. They enveloped us.

That constitutes a fantastic drain on anyone. It drained me of worldliness, and it drained me physically of my energy. To give up the material side and enter the spiritual realm at every performance can be devastating, but it is absolutely irresistible. "The thing" became stronger and stronger until sometimes the draining made me fall. This is hard for many people to understand. All during *Dolly*, I worked around people and for people who never understood or accepted it.

This tremendous gift, this rapport that spells success springs from a source I will not search for. The source has sought me. I only acknowledge that I am blessed and grateful.

And so one night, not long after *Dolly* opened, when I was living at the Willard Hotel in Washington, D.C. (down the street from the National Theater and across from the White House), this acclaim, adulation, love became so strong that I sat down and decided to write another book. It would be a book about all the things one can learn and feel across the footlights. Across that bridge we see and live all emotions. With our people out there, we smile, shake, shudder, scream, pray, and amaze. There comes a time when we awaken, when we see the other side. For me, it is an awakening that has not ceased and will not cease.

Pearl Bailey

P.S.

I find that I automatically try to classify my insights and my experiences according to what emotions or feelings are associated. At times, as you read this book, you will say that Pearl has repeated her thoughts. That is true, but at each writing I strike from a different point in time and under the influence of different emotions. I just know that something compels me to say some of these things over and over again. Truth is never repetitious. It gets stronger each time. Whenever truth is spoken there is somewhere an increase of understanding and faith. Therefore, truth must prevail even in repetition. So here it is—

Over and over again,
In love,
Pearl

Contents

Presidential appointment . . .

Greetings:

Reposing special trust and confidence in your integrity, prudence, and ability, I hereby appoint you Ambassador of Love to the entire world, authorizing you hereby to do and perform all such matters and things as to the said place or office do appertain or as may be duly given you in charge hereafter.

RICHARD M. NIXON

Ambassador of Love

Frank Borman brought three Russian cosmonauts and their interpreter to see *Dolly* (the White House, no, but *Dolly*, yes). Before the show a decision had been made, based on security procedures, that these men could not go up to the stage but could only be introduced from the audience.

I got them up there anyway. What the heck, sitting there with people all around them, I figured they were in worse danger than they might be on the stage. Actually, they were having such a ball, they could have been shot without feeling it, at least for the moment.

One of them was a big boy, really big, and a charmer. All of them were friendly, warm, and extremely cordial. We had many laughs standing up there. I had studied in the afternoon and learned to say "how are you," "I love you," and "you're welcome" in Russian. My Russian wasn't good, you understand, but decent. It was a kind of Southern Russian. As they turned to leave the stage, I kissed Frank. As they were all climbing down, the big Russian charmer said something to the other two. I stopped the interpreter and asked, "What did he say?" "He said, 'You kissed the American astronaut, but not him.'" I called the big guy back to the stage, and he stood there on the edge while I smothered him with kisses. He was definitely a Beautiful Red Russian. He left, full of love and kisses from an American.

One Goes Up and One Goes Down

I know many people who are Arab and many people who are of the Hebrew faith. It has occurred to me that the Hebrew gesture goes down—it's head, mouth, and heart. The Arabs go the other way—heart, mouth, then head.

Not long ago, I happened to be talking to two businessmen in the West—one Arab and one Jewish. I said, "You know, you people just amaze me. It's the funniest thing in the world. At this point your people are fighting like hell. It's just like your gestures. One goes up and one goes down. Why in the hell don't you all meet in the middle and talk?" What I really meant was when you get to the mouth, why don't you just stop that hand and talk for a while?

Let Humanity Operate

I met the wonderful actress Ruth Warrick while I was playing in *Dolly*. We became good friends. One day as she was about to leave town, I asked her to see *The Great White Hope*. Some time later, I got the following letter:

Dearest Sister Pearl,

Twice I missed you at the theatre yesterday. That's because I took your advice and saw "The Great White Hope" and had a conversation with Mr. Jones after the show. He is fantastic and the show is an unforgettable experience. "How white are you going to be?" is so scathing, I cannot imagine anyone failing to see the sick, sick, sick inanity of racist idiocies! Thank God most young people are too hip to be caught up in that hypocrisy. Even the young militants don't frighten me too much. I've had them scream "white witch" at me one minute and the next, forget and laugh and joke, because humanity is stronger than bigotry. You spoke of your horror over the picture of the students with guns on the campus, but did you see the picture on the front page of the Times this morning Thursday 24th. It's of the President of Cornell, Perkins, Eric Evans, the Afro American leader, and David Bunak, the S.D.S. leader, all smiles, relaxed comradely communication smiles. The young militants are not smirking with victory or gloating. There is joyous human togetherness in their faces, with no one faction the victors but everyone the winners. I may be inaccurately optimistic, but I believe as you do that love is stronger than hate. And the feelings that pull humanity together are stronger than those which pull us apart. All that is needed is enough "openness" on both sides to allow this humanity to operate. When people catch on how much greater it feels to love than hate, they'll kick that stupid habit. Some of the young coloreds will be militants for a while to give themselves assurance that they are men, standing up for themselves as men who cannot be second class citizens. But they don't really want a separate society. Not most of them, not for long. Give them a place in the action, and they'll not be so "exclusive" for long. They won't buy all the hypocrisy that's been too long a part of our society, for that's good. You and I don't really buy it either. I know some hating black militants, and I know some beautiful brilliant militants, who sincerely believe they are helping us all to be free and I for one believe it. That's what they are doing at the universities. They are forcing the administration, the faculty, and the students to look into themselves. As President Perkins said, each faction has been going along completely without contact with the other. Each in its own little world because he was ignoring all the other people outside the cage. They meant absolutely nothing to him.

I went everyday to see him, and we went through the same routine. I always wore the red scraf under my hat. Then came the supreme moment. About the fifth day, he looked at me and started to pant, like a person gasping for breath. His big chest was heaving up and down. Then he put his hand over his heart and looked directly into my eyes like he was showing me how much he loved me. As I left, he watched me walk up the hill. Every few steps, I would stop, turn, and wave back at him. He stared me out of sight.

About a year later, Peetney and I went through Central Park. As we went into the Ape House, quite a few people were standing by the railing. It seemed to me that this ape was even bigger than the one in Seattle.

I was carrying a chocolate ice that Peetney had bought me. Immediately, as I walked up to the railing, the gorilla's eyes meet mine. (Heavens, could he be the brother of my Seattle friend?) I started thinking about it. What was this ape attraction? He completely lost awareness of everyone else. He came to the corner of the cage to get as close to me as he could, and just sat there staring at me. Love—it hit him. I said, "Do you want some ice?"

He held his hand outside the cage as if to reach for my hand. I said, "Oh no, I'm not going to hand it to you. Your fingers are too strong. You might grab the ice and me too."

His eyes got sad and he pulled his hand back into the cage. Then he seemed to get an idea. He started looking around the floor of his cage, and finally picked up a piece of carrot, smelled it, and looked at me. He seemed to say, "See, I have eaten of this, so you should have some too." Then he threw it to me. All the while, the female in the cage ignored all of this, and he certainly ignored her. I picked up the carrot and threw it back to him. He started to throw it again, but dropped it outside his cage.

I said, "See, you've lost the ball." His eyes grew sad again. I asked, "Do you still want this ice?" He stuck his hand out immediately. We continued to play and communicate in our way.

A lady walked up with some children, very small ones, to get a closer look. I got distracted because I was trying to keep the smallest child from getting too close to the ape. Some mothers really amaze me. This one was letting her three-year-old lean over the railing and reach playfully toward this huge ape. Finally the ape started to reach toward him. I couldn't stand it any longer. I said, "Oh, don't let him do that, dear. If this gorilla gets that child's hand, he could tear his arm from its socket trying to pull him into the cage. Please make him get down." The silly woman turned to this three-year-old child and said, "Did you hear what the lady said?" I mumbled, "Darling, never mind if he heard it, for heaven's sakes, did *you*?" It burned me up. I cannot understand women who do careless things like this. I see them all the time, sauntering across streets with a little child in front of them or behind them, not even holding hands.

They wandered away, and I returned to my friend on the other side of the bars. By this time, he had found another carrot. I finished eating the ice, and held up the cup. "It's all gone, I can't offer you anymore. Besides, I've got to leave," I told him. I got the distinct impression that he understood me. He looked at me in sheer disgust, then quickly picked up an old dirty carrot and dipped it in dirty water. He wasn't angry, he was just acting like any man, showing off a little bit, and acting tough. Really, he was flirting and thinking to himself, "I'm pleasing this broad with my antics. Now she's leaving. I got no ice. I'll fix her."

By this time the ape and I were beginning to draw a crowd. He got that carrot as wet as he could in that dirty water, and started toward the bars. I said, "Oh no you don't! Don't you dare throw that dirty thing at me." Then he reached and got an old wet lettuce leaf and threatened me again. I said, "No sir, I'm leaving." He looked at me for a moment and then dropped all of this stuff. He seemed to say, "Well, I have lost her anyway." I walked away a few steps and then turned to look back over my shoulder. Then it happened—m-m-m POW! He threw me a big kiss. Love, ah love! One day I must go back and see him again.

Still another time, I went to Jungle Land. I had the kids with me and it was 110° so we were not in the mood for lots of romance with the apes. We wanted to get home pretty soon. I stepped up to see the gorilla and threw him a few kisses. (Old flirty Pearl.) Then I said good-bye and started to leave. Then, WHAM! He had gotten a mouthful of spit together and had let loose right at me. I ducked. He missed me. The keeper said, "That's funny. The only time he does that is when his love interests don't work out."

To See Without Seeing

The show was over; I was enjoying my quiet moment. The manager appeared and said that a twelve-year-old girl, blind, wanted to meet me. Dear God. She came in, sort of running with her hands outstretched. As if to ask, "Where is she, where is she?" "Here, here." She found me.

I was awed by her presence as she ran her tiny sensitive fingers all over my face, weighed my jewelry, laughing quietly all the while, learning more about me than perhaps I know about myself. We talked and held onto each other for a beautiful few minutes. Never had I been so much in contact with one whose sight was gone.

To this girl and to me came sight, light, and complete awareness. For me, there was revelation that most of us look at humanity every day, but do not see except in shades of skin, position, and creed. It might be much better if we all had to feel a man's face with our hands, to search out his heart without first looking. To find a stranger's truth is slower this way, but more certain, and there is that excitement that comes with it.

Colors

A six-year-old girl, daughter of one of the performers in *Dolly*, came into my dressing room with a saying that she had just discovered—"Black is Beautiful." She came out with it just like that. The little girl was a regular visitor to my dressing room, but I had never heard her talk about things like this. She came in, often as not, because I had some candy and some ready love for her. She talked very wisely and brilliantly for her age.

Well, I suspected that the child had picked up the slogan without fully understanding its meaning. I said, "Sweetheart, everything that God makes is beautiful; every color that God makes is beautiful." She looked at me a little puzzled. Then she looked at the red rug on the dressing-room floor and suddenly said, "You know what, this red rug is beautiful, isn't it?" And I said, "Yes."

She turned that wonderful little face of hers to me and

said, "You know, I guess everything that God made is beautiful, no matter what color it is."

"Yes."

Then she belted out a beauty. "Miss Bailey, some babies don't even read the labels on crayons, do they?" That has to be one of God's gems.

When a child first starts to color with crayons, he reaches out for whatever colors he can get. His little paintings come out, at least to him, perfect masterpieces. There is no thought of matching or separating colors. Complete freedom there. Then they do not criticize their own work. They simply enjoy it as is.

Dem Days Are Over

I try to work the Shoreham Hotel every summer. It's an outdoor stage. The spot is beautiful with a fountain and all, but there is some heavy competition from the moon. Very few performers have a style that will play well in that huge outdoor space. If you can hold folks' attention out there, you've got it made. The Shoreham is the easiest job in show business too. Five days of work a week—unheard of in vaudeville. There's a nice swimming pool for the daytime, and about two hundred kids there to ask me questions. I regularly open the pool at ten A.M. and close it at eight P.M. Then I do one show, starting at ten at night. That's living for vaudevillians. It's almost like working in Europe.

I made many friends there. Some people I see year after year. They have a way of calling out to me during the show, "Hi, Pearl, how's the pool?" Or sometimes, "How are your feet now, Pearl?" I always kibbitz back and forth and work the whole thing into my act. The people love it and I find it enjoyable too. I remember one night, though, I heard a man with a big Southern drawl and a nip too many holler out to me, "Sing 'Dem Golden Chairs.' " In fact, the way he did it, it wasn't a request, it was more like an order. The attitude and the tone of the thing were unlike what I was used to hearing.

"Sorry, I don't know 'Dem Golden Chairs.' "

"You should," he shot back. (I knew, of course, what he wanted to hear, but I thought, "What the hell, let's enjoy him and have a smile." I turned his way again and talked to him like a little child. The audience was starting to love it. "Dearheart, I don't know 'Dem Golden Chairs.' I think what you want is 'Them Golden Slippers.' By the way, I spell that word, T-H-E-M, not D-E-M." The audience broke up, and so did this guy from the South. While they were still laughing, I started to sing "Oh, them golden slippers . . ." very slowly and thoughtfully. Did you ever hear that song done that way?

There's a nervous laughter
in the world . . .

Trust

America has grown old too fast. Our people ask questions we cannot answer anymore, because we have started to lie. We have lied and lied and lied to ourselves and to one another. Now it seems that we don't know right from wrong. We cannot free ourselves.

We cannot lie any longer by telling ourselves that we are free and democratic people. We cannot send men to fight just wars when they are at war with each other at home. We cannot tell ourselves that our children play happily when they spit on their fingers and rub each other to see if skin color will come off. We cannot tell ourselves that we have a civilized nation when we cannot accept civilization as a whole with all its people. The idea of separate but equal is a lie. The idea of separation contradicts our earliest ideals. We must look at our society as it is.

Many cultural influences coincide in our society. Right now we are adopting some of the ways of the Indians in wearing moccasins, beautiful headbands and beads. We are adopting the way of the Africans with hair standing nineteen feet high. And the way of John the Baptist with our flowing robes. And the Egyptians with our coats of many colors. The English, the Romans—all—yes, we are a nation of mixtures. Yet we can't seem to recognize each strand for its beauty. Temporarily, we adopt this and adopt that.

We are forever adopting while making nothing permanent. All has become temporary.

Youngsters seem to feel it most strongly. They look for symbols of this established lie, and show their anger in violence. Little children and young people in cellars and on rooftops are making bombs. Sometimes the poor unfortunate things blow themselves to bits. They turn on the television and they see our "intelligentsia," our great statesmen and orators, and they see immediately that a lot of these men are "out of it," away from the scene. They see some of the representatives of our establishment telling deliberate lies, and they look in their faces praying that they will stop. They look around them and see their cities in decay, and they see their leaders blaming it on one another. The silent majority, the loud minority—no one does anything to help. We rant, rave, riot, burn, snipe, hang. Our police and our courts have lost their position in the eyes of the young. They no longer trust a judge, and the judge no longer trusts them. They don't trust a policeman. And lord knows, many policemen don't trust them. It is one, big, beautiful world of mistrust. And still we lie.

Those few who do want to do something constructive about our country are quickly submerged by that big group (oh, it's really a large group) that says it's all right, because tomorrow we're going to form a committee, don't worry. When the committee is formed, it turns out to be as full of crap as the one formed three days before.

God created us all. For heaven's sake, buy part of that. Someone or something larger than us had something to do with our being. In love, we were created. If man continues in the path that he has carved for himself, his destruction is assured. He will reach that ultimate end. Americans are afraid now, even walking the streets. We lock our doors,

and if we step into an elevator we don't know whether we'll
make it out alive. The hope for a political solution is a slim
one. Several men form a ticket, make promises, and we vote.
After a while in office, they are confusing one another, accusing one another, and mistrusting everyone. And while
they sit there in their greed, mistrust, and lust for power,
they can destroy a whole city, and city after city.

We don't need prophets. The handwriting is there in
every man's language. "Love one another—love one another."

Echoes

On Virginia Graham's TV show, the discussion turned to
the ill-treatment of the Indians, and eventually included the
war, atrocities, and most of the evils of the world. The lady
presenting her theories was Miss Jane Fonda. She said that
it was high time that we concerned ourselves about the Indians, for in a certain sense they really are more American
than the rest of us. I agree with that. I'm not sure that when
we started across the continent with our covered wagons,
these people were automatically unfriendly to us. They were
only strangers, and we called them hostile.

Jane Fonda is quite a young lady—she seemed very sincere in what she was saying, and I really hope that she was.
Some of the people in the audience began to ask her serious
questions, and she was quite up to them. No one swayed her
from her convictions. Then an Indian stood up, introduced
himself, and made a strong statement. "We don't need a
white woman to lead us."

Wow! Virginia Graham really lit into him. "I don't think

that's necessary, that racial feeling." (I'll buy that, Virginia.) Fonda, herself, was quite taken back. This was a big blow to her cause. Then other Indians spoke, quite intelligently, about their people's thinking.

Almost everyone in America today speaks of the great hurt and harm and confusion of the minority groups. But until very recently, we didn't hear so very much about these Indian folks, who have been so mistreated for so many years. We simply haven't paid attention to their hunger, their lack of housing. They have lost their place in this world, and now we see them sitting on the side of the road asleep.

What this Indian man went on to say was, how long can you people stand outside and look into our lives without doing something, or at least letting us do something? Virginia asked him what he meant by that statement about a white woman leading the Indians. He spoke again, but politely ignored the question. Perhaps what he meant was that he is a man with dignity, and he should lead himself. I don't really think that he meant to say that he did not appreciate her concern. His face on that screen showed his goodness and his emotions. There was an anger, barely concealed, that came from his heart.

Miss Fonda and the Indian agreed on one thing. Both felt that as a nation we were looked upon originally as constructive people and freedom lovers—that we had worked and given of ourselves, given dreams to other people and nations. Both felt that we had destroyed that in the Vietnam War, through the treatment of Indians, etc. The Indian pointed out that before the settlers arrived, Indians had a culture that meant something to them. They had dignity and pride. The settlers, crossing in their wagons and claiming new land, slaughtered the Indians because they were in the way. Pioneers took away the wealth of the Indians and destroyed their dreams. We seemed always to think we had reasons for doing that. Weren't we, after all, building a country? What we failed to consider was that we were destroying our country at the same time. We have always asked the Indian to accept our ways, yet we could not accept his.

The Indian on the show said, "The young Indians will no longer take it." Then, in essence, he said, "We are a minority, true. But we are determined to see some of our dreams realized." I am sure that he meant he wanted to be recognized as a human being. I found myself wanting to speak directly to him through the television set. At that moment I wanted to say, "Sir, there will be many Americans of other minorities who will stand by your side. Not everyone, so don't depend on that. Our country has sent us to many other lands to fight for freedom for other people, yet many of us are enslaved at home. Our country is usually among the first to help when there is an earthquake anywhere in the world, or a flood, or any other disaster, and yet we have disaster in our own land. We send tons of food and equipment, medicine, nursing, while in this country people are standing around literally with their tongues hanging out in need of these things."

Lady Bird Johnson campaigned to make America beautiful. She was concerned mostly with planting flowers and trees and picking up litter. Sure, lots of people laughed, but some of her projects have indeed been lovely contributions to life. We need to go beyond that now. We need to concern ourselves with thoughts and with materials—make of them flowers and plant them all around the country.

Now we are all crying, crying about petty, selfish things. We take the short view and scream our lungs out about personal inconvenience and little disappointments of the present. Soon, by God, I pray that we will all get so hoarse that we will lose our voices. We will open our lips, but nothing will come out. We will be forced to listen to the echoes of what we have done.

There is no search involved. Truth is evident. The sun is on the other side, and we have only to cross over. It's as simple as that. Real happiness is love, is completion.

Yes, the Indians want something. Yes, Jane Fonda, I hope they get it. I am sad to see youth so sad. I am ashamed because I know that we who are older should have done what was right before they had a chance to get this sad.

My Country 'Tis Of Thee

A Responsive Reading

My Country 'Tis Of Thee

> Our country—then let all mankind share in its beauty and glory.

Sweet Land Of Liberty

> Today we are asking ourselves, is it sweet? and for whom is the liberty?

Of Thee I Sing. . . .

> What song shall I sing? A hymn? Then it may be said we are too mournful. A joyful song? But are we really that happy?

★

Long May Our Land Be Bright

> Our land shall be bright with what? Blood or sunshine?

With Freedom's Holy Light

> Which freedoms? The ones God gave or the one man devises?

Protect Us By Thy Might

> Are we really asking for God's protection? Aren't man's weapons mighty?

Great God Our King

> Now we acknowledge Him and call Him King, and yet each day we disobey our Ruler. When we awaken to ourselves and start to live as He directs us, then we will be able to sing our song with clear hearts.

In Common

Trees growing in the forest,
Each in its place;
Some leaning on others' shoulders,
But all with roots in earth.
They have things in common—
The Above and the Below.
Men standing like trees,
Yet not believing it so.

The Night the Government Stopped

Men in grey suits fairly burst through the backstage door. Everyone was startled. We didn't know what was going on. Then I remembered that Liz Carpenter had called to say that President Johnson was considering visiting *Hello, Dolly!* One of the men came into my dressing room with the manager, Mr. Kirkpatrick. The agent just stayed at the door. I don't know yet what that was for.

After intermission, there was a stir in the audience. I got word that they were putting up four seats in the aisle, because the theater was packed. When the curtain came up, lo and behold, there he was, the President of the United States, with Lady Bird at his side. The other two, I suppose, were Secret Service men. There were Secret Service men in the wings too, and everyplace. I thought to myself, "Well, somehow I'm going to get him up on the stage." From where I stood, there was the front edge of the stage, then an orchestra pit covered by a net, so that dancers could leap across. And then a narrow, curving runway that reached out into the audience. It had taken me quite a while to get used to working on that narrow runway. Anyway, at the end of the show, folks, your President came up there.

Now I have to wear glasses for reading and sewing, but I never wear them on the stage. I simply had that runway memorized. When the President and Mrs. Johnson came on the stage through the side exit, the Secret Service men went out of their minds. No protection up there. I took Lady Bird's hand. Now she didn't have her glasses on either. She reached back and got the President's hand, and he didn't have his glasses either. The three of us, blind leading the blind, went tripping out the runway. Ladies and gentlemen, for fifteen minutes your country was in trouble.

On the Train

I am sad to think that many young people have never traveled on a train. It is a thrill to ride along and enjoy the countryside—not to rise so far above the earth. Once as I headed West, this came:

Snow on the ground,
Sun on the mountain tops,
Shadows on the plain.
Two gas stations
Five hundred miles apart;
Horses and cows grazing
On greenish-brown grass.

A lonely station stop—
The West.

Montana

Today God let me see his work,
And a million times more I asked—
How did he do it?
Not why.

Pennsylvania

Fall colors kiss
The Pennsylvania Turnpike
As I drive, it is no longer

A highway.
It is God showing Michelangelo
What He meant—
Without a brush.

Politicians

I find that politicians are able to fool the public better than actors can. It isn't that they act better, it's just that they have a nonpaying audience standing there hoping for something—promises that can never be kept by one man. And politicians do spout promises. Their fists bang the table, their faces turn red (embarrassed by their own lies?).

As soon as a politician wins he forgets audiences, free or paid, and starts to listen to himself. What he hears sounds pretty good to him. As soon as he loses, he remembers the audiences, paying and nonpaying, and hates them. Then he aligns himself with the winner and starts to agree with him, whom he just finished calling liar. Oh Lord!

Celebrity Power

There are people outside waiting for us to help, to speak, then take sides and lead the cause. The celebrity has a large power over men's minds and activities today. Actually, I feel very good about the fact that many celebrities have been able to do some good and get into things they weren't thought bright enough to do before. For the celebrities themselves, there are some pitfalls to watch out for.

We have to make sure that when we take sides we're doing so for the right reason, not because we're after more silver and gold. Some celebrities are accustomed to making their decisions on the basis of financial gain to themselves. When you're talking about causes and movements, this won't do.

For a celebrity, there isn't much difference between going along with the thing and leading it. The effect can be very much the same. Therefore, we really have to pay attention. Movements for social reforms of various kinds require and deserve real commitment from people. Celebrities who just go along with things are really playing at concern for their fellow man. It is up to us to stop and think the situation over so that we can be sure in our own hearts that we are giving ourselves to something good rather than something that will be bad for people.

I have observed that people are very much influenced by my thoughts. I think about that a lot. That keeps me from jumping on any band wagon that comes my way. I watch out particularly for those with the greased wheels. More than once I have been disillusioned by people who speak out for one cause, get an army trailing behind them, and then allow things to go to pieces. The people who are following down the path begin to split up among themselves. They become divided and confused, straggling all over the highway. Soon they are stumbling over each other, and the next thing you know, men are being stepped on. If you look back from the head of the ranks, you see no army at all, but rather disruption. The key is that when some of these leaders look back and see disruption, they turn around in their tracks and walk roughshod right back over the backs of their followers. In their confusion, these people may look up asking for water, bread, bandages for their wounds, but these leaders keep going. Their motive then is to round up another army on the excuse that the old one failed.

More Angry Than Frightened

There's a nervous laughter in the world.
Say something, absolutely nothing, and people giggle—
Never even hearing what's been said.
They're afraid again—
Of themselves.

Where is this frightening life leading us now? Every day we try to talk it out with ourselves and with others. Why, why are we destroying ourselves and others? The bombs are falling. Not on Germany, not on Japan, Korea, Vietnam —they're falling in our land, and we are throwing them.

Tear down the school, kill the children, kill the policemen, kill, kill. Bomb that building. Use this drug. Long dresses. Short dresses. Kidnap. Hijack. Hatred is rampant. I remember them walking down the street, holding up two fingers to give the peace sign. At what price, children? The flower child—where did he go? Where are the love youngsters who were going to try to understand so we could have a happier world? Now I hear folks say, "Don't get involved." I say that we must all get involved, or there will be no more happy children, no schools to go to, no safety in the streets, no human possibilities. Let the skyscrapers fall where they may?

What are we going to do? Now policemen walk in fear and many in hatred. Can law and order prevail? Is this some new era? We seldom stop these days to look around at the handiwork of the Master. He's had a few things to say lately. Every time we do one of our monstrosities, he tops it, and we're so lost in ourselves that we cannot see what he has done. If we tear down a building, he creates an earthquake and swallows our small destruction. We wipe out a few people with a gun, and a tornado levels an entire town.

I'm afraid that even if we stopped war in this country, we would find more war in other countries. New leaders and old leaders alike play politics here and there. No one is going anyplace, and we lie.

The love children started out digging each other. They saw each other simply as members of a common cause against an establishment. Now it seems the children, dear God, are frightened of each other. Lightning has struck. The children will save us?

Let us go ahead and end it all if we must, and then let us start from the ashes again. What would we rebuild upon? That's the major issue, and it should be.

I'm not as frightened as I am angry—angry at myself and others for not preserving what God gave us with love.

I shall take heart
When nervous laughter fades,
When strangers can smile, with neither asking why,
    lock their hands and hearts—
And understand.

I am beginning to see what soul searching means—to be able to see ourselves, past and present. Every time we find one thing in ourselves to be perfected and work on it, we cannot help but see more perfection in others.

Egotism

A friend of mine who is not in show business asked me whether at any time in my career I had enjoyed feeling like a big shot. I worked very hard for some years, after all, to reach a position in show business that you could call successful. "Didn't you ever just look at yourself and feel that you really were hot stuff, a real big shot? Did you ever try it?"

Mama told me that I had talent from the beginning of me. Perhaps I did get a little haughty sometimes or strut a little more than I should have. It happens. Even yet, for a minute now and then. Yesterday I went out to do a little shopping. Walking down the street, I got an inside feeling about how nice it is—nice to hear people say as I pass, "Ah, there she goes." Or, "There she is." Sometimes that seems to be a wonderful sound. Still, I hope that my headiness never comes on as strong as with some.

Peetney said to me that she would like to see God. I said, "You see Him every day, you just sometimes may not recognize Him." As I was talking to her, I realized that one thing that keeps me honest is my strong intuition for people. Almost as if by séance, I have always been able to (and here's that word) *recognize* the truth about people, even people I don't know. There are some kinds of radiation that let me know people for what they are. I don't always like it. Most of the time I try to do something about it. Sometimes this works to my joy and sometimes it works to my sorrow. Whichever, it helps to remove selfish pride. When I meet a person, it isn't that I decide to form an opinion of him. I know him at once—invariably—I recognize much in him, and he doesn't know how I do it. Sometimes when I reveal what I recognize, people accuse me of trying to play God. That is not it at all. All I want to do is to help bring out all the goodness that I see.

When attention is turned to me, that also removes headiness. Although you might not expect it to be so, when people stare at me or want to touch me, it takes away the headiness. I recognize it for what it is. And I recognize me for what I am.

I went to see *Forty Carats* the other night. Waiting outside before the show, I sat down on a three-way fire pipe that comes out of the front of the building. It was a warm night, and E.B., who was going to the theater with me, had stepped down to the corner to get me a Pepsi Cola. I had picked up the tickets and then, spying this fire pipe, had decided to sit down. Most of the people walking by didn't recognize me. For one thing, I had on a big floppy hat that made it hard for people standing up to see my face. Once in a while, though, someone would peep under the hat and say, "That's her, that's her." Now call it fame or whatever you want, you've got to feel pretty queer with someone lifting your hatbrim, peeping, and dropping it back down. That's not about to make you feel like a big shot. Actually, it can make you feel silly. I'd just look up and smile at them, and occasionally, I'd push the brim up myself to watch for E.B. and that Pepsi Cola. Finally, I got tired of the whole thing and pushed the whole brim back completely.

Now the people knew me. "Hi, Pearl." A lady came by, put her face not beside mine but in mine, if that's possible. "How are you, Pearl?" I said, "Fine."

"You feeling better?"

"Yes, I am." She went away for a minute, then came back and asked me again. I said, "Yes, I am, but you just asked me that."

"Yes, I know, but I just wanted to be sure." As she was

leaving, I turned my head and found myself nose-to-nose with another lady who said, "Can I ask you a question?" Could she ask a question! Lord, we could have kissed!

She said, "This may sound silly, but why are you sitting on that pipe?"

I looked up at her and with my eyes only, I questioned her manners, her sanity, and her kindness. I said, "Why, I am sitting here just because I want to sit on this pipe."

"Well," she said, "I think your face is so pretty." I thanked her and thought it was all over. But then she started again. "I'm just fascinated. I'd really like to know why you're on the pipe." By now, the whole sidewalk was filled with people staring at me sitting there. I said, "Dear lady, I'm sitting here because I am a human being and I would like to sit on this pipe." A man overheard and said, "Good, I'll sit down with you." And he did.

"Frankly, folks," I told them, "I'm waiting for my friend to bring me a soda." Now the Production Manager from the show came out the stage entrance and asked if I wanted to sit backstage. I said, "No, son." And then I changed my mind.

As I was about to stand up a man said, "You know what you look like, Pearl?" (I thought, here it comes, he's going to say I look like a perfect ass.) ". . . You look like an American Indian sitting there."

"Well, I'm part Indian, mister, so that helps, huh?"

A woman said, "Isn't that like a child?"

"I hope I am, lady."

"No, Miss Bailey (the same woman's voice), I was talking about this child." I turned. It was a little boy selling flavored ice from a cart. He had let the woman know that he would like to give me a free ice, but was afraid to make the offer himself. The funny thing is that the little boy didn't really know who I was, but he liked me and he had heard me say I was waiting for my Pepsi.

"Who are you, lady?"

"Pearl, darling."

"Would you like a free ice?"

"Thanks." I promised to send him a book. Then E.B. showed up and I took my little pointed cup of ice into the theater.

Once inside and seated, I noticed a lady in my row who had turned completely sideways in her seat in order to stare at me. Now that can be a bit too much after a while. I consider it just a little rude. The entire time she was staring at me, I sort of wiggled. She made me feel very uncomfortable. Then her husband stood up and faced the theater audience and said, "Anybody want my autograph?" Under my breath, I said to E.B., "Why in the hell doesn't he sit down and stop being silly." The man in front of me heard the statement and whispered back, "I agree." You see, the point was that all of this attention wasn't thrilling. It was only embarrassing. All the while, I was trying to get rid of my chocolate ice before curtain time. I squeezed the cup and finished the chocolate. Now what was I going to do with the cup, with everybody watching? Lawdy, if I threw it down, everybody would think, "That dirty entertainer." I folded it up finally, and E.B. took it to the lobby for me.

Zsa Zsa Gabor, who is the star of the show, is a good friend of mine. You have to know Zsa Zsa well to fully enjoy her. This is a magnetic woman full of fire and warmth. Zsa Zsa and I call each other "Sister." I always kid the Gabors and say that I'm the fourth one. Zsa Zsa, Magda, Eva, then me, the one they don't talk about. She was wonderful in the show, and so were the others in the cast. At the end, she beckoned me up to the stage. Tom Poston and some of the others helped me get up there. We put on a little perform-ance and the theater really went wild. It was my pleasure to take bows with that fine cast. I was thinking to myself, "Wow, in *Dolly* almost every night I had performers, ath-letes, dignitaries—yes, even Presidents—up on the stage after the show. Now here I am doing what they did." It felt funny and good to be in front of an audience, because I had not performed for two whole months.

Outside the dressing room and in the alleyway, a great many people were after us for autographs. A few of them came to me first, but I told them to get Zsa Zsa's because after all, she was the star of the show. Come to think of it, I very seldom go backstage, but it seemed natural in this case. I think it's nice when special friends come backstage after a performance, but knowing how tired you can get, I often write a nice note instead and send it back with a mes-senger. When a performer has given so much on the stage and is worn out, it can be a little too much to get hung up in that close dressing room. Also, as you know, I believe that whether a performance has been good or bad, one needs a few moments with God to talk it over afterward.

When we got to Forty-fifth Street, E.B. touched my arm and said, "Do something for this little girl, she keeps tug-ging at your sleeve." I looked at her and asked, "What's the matter, honey, did I forget to autograph your program?" She said, "Yes," but kept crying. I would guess that she was all of twelve years old and the tears really were streaming down her face. A number of people had stopped to watch this scene. I bent down and put my arms around her shoul-der and asked, "What are you crying for?" I felt kind of helpless because even her feet were trembling, and her little body was racked with sobbing.

I lowered my head so that she could whisper to me. "Miss

Bailey, I never thought I'd get close enough to touch you, and now I have." What a funny feeling, but beautiful. I really think it just isn't possible to get selfish and proud over a thing like that. Things like that happened all the time when I was Dolly. The people would reach out to touch and kiss the hem of my finale dress.

After a pause I said, "Are you going to be an actress?"

"Oh, yes," she said.

"Then, darling, be a good one."

With that, she started getting all upset again, and she answered, "I will, but I still just can't believe I'm here with you." We chatted, exchanged addresses, and I hope to continue my contact with this little friend. I dried her eyes and turned to look at a lady who had been observing it all. Then I realized that the woman was her mother. She had not attempted to touch our friendship, sensing our love all the time.

Many, many times, such things have happened. People, strangers, want to touch, to kiss, to come near. It happens without particular regard to race, creed, color, or sex. It comes from some intuitive sense of loving, and whenever it happens, I find it humbling. Far from inspiring me to feel conceit, it has almost exactly the opposite effect on me. It seems to mean the most when it happens with children, maybe because of my special love for them. I have come to think of children as "Little Jesus People."

Ego

Most people assume that performers float around in an ego balloon. Why do they think so? Is it because we walk on the stage and give everyone a chance to stare up at us? Is it because we give others a chance to say, "Look at her up there, showing off her wares, so sure of herself." What about you people in the audience? Aren't you out there all dressed up in your finery for others to see? Aren't you showing off your wares? Or did you come only to stare at the show-offs who have the gall to stand up front and portray life for you? Are you wholly concerned with those who stand up there, deliver, walk off, come back, bow, and seem to say (some of them), "Kiss my ass, I did it." (I've seen that kind.) Did you come just to see those who throw kisses with both hands yet, and look as though they're begging for your mercy? They are the ones for whom your applause is usually thin and polite. Those who feel they did not give enough and now must beg for your mercy, they wish for just enough applause to get off that stage.

Do you know what those spotlights do to you? They frighten a person, awaken him, they make him know he's on. We performing puppets move to those invisible strings that audiences hold. Some of us are held by ropes, some by chains, others by threads. And still others are just dangling, because they have broken their threads. You are the puppeteers.

You, my dears, must let your ego tell you to tell us when we are good or bad (and don't, don't forget that we have to listen for your judgment). You open and close the curtains on our careers. Can we be egotists?

When one is truly blessed with a great talent, it's true that he moves to his own strings. The fiddler plays his own tune, the dancer dances his own rhythm. A fine talent in true harmony with an audience must lose feelings of egotism. The reason is that he is receiving a gift. There is an ego in that but it is not the sort that makes you think you're better than someone else. To stand there and deliver, good or bad, does not require ego. It requires guts.

Yes, of course, there are some egomaniacs around our business. But in my experience, I've found most of them among the people who stand back and say, "I created this artist." Now the true artist knows that he has been created, but he also knows by Whom. Only the artist molded by man's commercial hand needs ego. How else could he make it?

What is ego anyway? Is it the idea that you are going to be the best or that you are the best already? There is a kind of ego struggle then between a performer and his audience. Often, I suspect that a performer thinks he's better than his audience or vice versa. You see, if an audience refuses to applaud a performer, the performer can take his ego offstage and say to himself and a few friends, "How lousy you were out there in the audience." That works the other way too. A disappointed audience always faults the performer.

What we typically call an egotistical man is really a frightened human being, begging for recognition. No true artist needs ego in that sense. He needs love. He needs his talent. He needs a job. And he needs guts, but he does not need egotism. He needs only to satisfy others for his own satisfaction. That is not ego; that is love.

Selfishness

There are some people in the world who say that no matter what you do you're looking out for yourself. Even if you do something that seems to be unselfish, you are really trying to make yourself feel better. I ask myself, is self-sacrifice possible or not? Of course, you can sacrifice yourself accidentally. Does that count or not? I am working on this one, but I cannot seem to come to an answer.

A masochist is selfish. I can think of times when I have punished myself selfishly. Knowing a man cared, I have hurt myself in order to hurt him. Actually, I do not delight in being hurt, so I guess I miss being a masochist by about an inch. If I hurt myself in order to get sympathy, love from him, then I miss being a masochist by a little. Still, I am selfish.

There is a lot of selfishness in show business. I notice it most often when someone comes to me to persuade me to do something—sign a contract, play a certain club, etc. Almost always they open by telling me how great it's going to be for me. That's the story of my life. The fact is that it's about six to one that if I co-operate it's going to be very good for the guy who is trying to persuade me.

I have two friends who almost get insane when I refuse to stop whatever I am doing and satisfy the public. All kinds of motives come into play. Maybe they want to bring someone into my dressing room. If I refuse, which I sometimes do, then I may get a little pressure. It's a combination of things. My friends are proud of me, and want their guests to meet me. Maybe my friends are showing off a little and are afraid that their own guests will think badly of them if they don't get into the room. Sometimes it just seems that they want me to pay back a debt for them. Sometimes the pressure and the mixture of motives have led me to feel bitterness toward these people, yet I do love them.

It is just that once too often they intruded into my silent moment of depth after I had given everything in a performance. They became selfish, and I resented it more from them because they knew me well and should have understood what I needed after a long performance. Something in me always rises up to say, "This moment is mine." Sometimes I would almost rather have people take away years of my life than take away a moment.

Rich Man, Poor Man, Beggar Man

Before *The Raw Pearl* some folks snickered when I said from the stage that I meant to write a book. I guess they figured I was a vaudevillian and it sounded a little far-fetched to think that I would try to be a writer too. The fact is that for people in my business, the name of the game is sharing. Performers have to be able to do a lot of different things. I'm not a seamstress, but I can sew on a button simply because I had to do it for many years. I'm not a hairdresser, and yet I did my own hair because for many years I couldn't afford to get anyone else to do it. During those lonely moments of being without a job, you learn. I learned needlepoint during the lonely times. And I learned to cook too on sterno stoves in small bathrooms of hotels years ago. I am not a diplomat by profession, but one learns diplomacy in our business fast.

Writing a book is another way for me to share. Performers learn that selfishness leads nowhere. Because at some point they realize that nothing belongs to them. That can be a big blow. A laborer can hold his pick and shovel and say, "This is mine." But a performer is not a performer without an audience.

Even when we step off the stage, drained of our energy, people insist that we share. Under those conditions, people have said to me, "You'd better be nice to me because we make your living." When I hear that, I tighten like a drum. "Make my living?" My bones are aching. But they are right. Without them, I am through, they say. If ever I cease to share with them, I am nothing, they say. The point is that we have to share because it is our instinct to do so, and not because someone has frightened us into it. My greatest difficulty is in finding the line between sharing as God intended and giving myself away entirely.

Nonlisteners

To talk to someone who does not listen is enough to tense the devil. I have found some people who really never listen to anyone. They hear only themselves, yet they can talk to someone else in their bag and there is apparent understanding. I think it is because neither one really listens to the other. These people get on so well together because they have nothing to disagree about.

God's Whole Hand

Every man thinks he is somebody. A few years ago, I almost forgot who I was through negative thinking. That was before I really let spirit fully emerge. My values were lying dormant, unused—my own fault.

Some things had happened that made me feel rejected. I felt unaccepted as a person and as a performer, and in addition I was physically ill.

It was not only that I felt unaccepted, it was that I actually felt unworthy of acceptance. A man's sense of personal worth fluctuates according to his insides sometimes. Maybe that is good too, for the scales not to stay so even all the time. Occasionally we need a judgment time for ourselves. Crisis and imbalance bring it about.

In my case, the scales went out of balance when I ceased to feel that people knew what I had to offer and what I wanted to give. The realization made me withdraw into a shell of inner-self and, in full retreat, I didn't even want to show people anymore. I felt that I had much to give, but no place, no way in which to give it. "Where do I put this thing that no one understands?" I placed no blame on race, religion, or creed, but I did go completely to the defensive.

When I entered the hospital in 1965, I had about twenty pounds too much weight on me. My doctor told me straight, "You're a wonderful-looking woman, but, lady, wake up. Come to yourself. Don't you know that you are somebody?" When I was under sedation, I became even more defensive. There was a constant sinking feeling. I came back at him with, "Doc, everybody is somebody." He answered, "But you're something special. God puts his finger on some, but he has put his whole hand on you."

To the tell the truth, since that day, I have felt much

more optimism and love. Since then I have known that I must use my right to give and receive love. I know that man can take nothing from me. He can neither give breath, nor take it away. I have come to think of myself as somebody with something to give. How nice. I shall bestow it as given. Man, take it or leave it. How man receives my gift is his concern. I shall just give in love.

Style

My friend Jeannie and I were at the ranch in Apple Valley. Louie and his band were working in Vegas at the Flamingo. Since Jeannie's husband Nick is in the band, we decided to drive up to see the boys. It was winter, so I decided to wear a new sable coat that I had bought. Very exciting!

Jeannie got all dressed up too and we went riding down the road, a big double-lane highway. A car drove up beside us and the people must have recognized me because they started waving like crazy. I wiggled my fingers playfully back at them, and they stayed right alongside. I fished around in my purse for a cigarette. But the pack was empty. I don't inhale cigarettes, so it's really a waste of time my smoking at all. Also, I never really finish a cigarette, and I have a habit of saving the butts. I pulled the pack out and mashed it, because I was just sure I was going to find a choice butt that I could resmoke.

Great! I managed to find one, all twisted and bent. After many tries, I got it lighted. Now I was really cute, waving the hand, bent cigarette in it. Jeannie got embarrassed. She said, "Sister, you should be ashamed of yourself. Here you are waving at these people in that sable coat and shooting butts. What must they think of you?"

I said, "How the hell do you think I got this coat? Shooting butts!"

Greenwich Village

Years ago I lived in Greenwich Village. And today I went back there just to look around. There have been some changes. When I lived there, the Village was all quiet. Today, when we turned a certain corner, there they were. So many of them that the street was blocked. Their hair was streaming and banjos were plunking. They seemed quite at peace with one another in their own little place. I was in the back seat with the window rolled down. Three or four kids peeped in the window. They seemed to be curious about this strange type with the long black car and the chauffeur. I stuck my hand out the window and waved them closer. Then a couple of them recognized me. "Ah, hello, Miss Bailey. Couldn't you get a larger car?" They weren't angry, but they did want to kid me a little bit. I put my hand to the side of my mouth like I wanted to whisper so the chauffeur wouldn't hear me. Then I leaned over and said, "The car is rented. I have to give it back in an hour." They broke up laughing and waved good-bye to me as we drove away. Farther down the street, I left the car entirely and had coffee and cake with the young.

That's Me

I was in Wolfe's in Miami Beach, sitting in a booth with my children. One of the owners was on the phone and a friend of his strolled over to the table. He started conversing with the children, then turned to me and said, "Your voice sounds so familiar and you look like someone I've seen before." I took the whole thing as a kind of joke. "Oh, do I really," I said, putting it on just a little bit.

"Oh yes, yes you definitely remind me of someone."

DeeDee popped up and said, "Don't you know who this is?"

I said, "Please don't say it, let's have some fun." Then I turned to him and said, "Okay, mister, now think."

"Oh, yes, I think I've got it. Only you're so much younger." Ah ha! Ha ho! (Blessings on thee, man.) Then he continued, "I just can't think of her name. She's a good bit older than you are, and she's on TV, movies, records— you wouldn't maybe know her name, would you?"

"Ah ha! I'm one of her biggest fans," I said. He followed with, "Whatever her name is, she's not as pretty, I know that." That did it. To hell with the suspense. "Is her name Pearl? Is that who you have in mind?"

"That's the one, lady, that's her."

"Kiss me, mister, I am she, her, and all that. I'm as old as you can imagine, yet younger than spring."

As if that hadn't been enough. A lady came up about two minutes later and said, "Pearl Bailey, I love you. I'm your biggest fan." Gee whiz, until that moment I had thought the other fellow was my biggest fan. This lady went on, ranting and raving. I got flustered and my delicious buttered bagel wouldn't go down. I almost choked on it.

"I've always wanted to meet you," she said, and then she hit me with it, "What do you do?"

Wow Wee!! All I could do was look at her. Finally I said, "What do you mean what do I do?"

"I mean sing? Dance? Act? Or what is it?"

Now I had to figure that this lady had maybe heard someone say that there I was and I was an entertainer of some kind. That was enough to bring her over.

"Madame, I do what I've been doing all along, don't you know?"

She answered sweetly, "I know you do something very good, and I like you—but what is it?"

I decided to make a point of it. I said, "Dearheart, you mean you came across this restaurant and gave me the great greeting, going crazy over me, and you don't even know what I do?"

I thought I had her at that point. But then she answered, "Well, Pearl, you see, I've been out of town for three or four months."

Evaluating Others

People are very curious about famous performers. They want to know everything. How do we eat, sleep, etc.? Some people think of us almost as queer creatures who live apart from others. The fact is that there is in us a need of humanity quite like everyone feels. In many ways, I envy the average man without fame more than he could envy me.

Underneath, all of us have some problems in common, whether we are famous or not. For example, we all have to figure out how to view others and we have to try to find truth about ourselves. The two problems are very much related. How can we recognize honesty in others if we are not ourselves honest? We need to be able to see whether a man is being dishonest with himself or with others or with both.

Throughout my career, I have spent a lot of time asking myself whether I set a standard of honesty and love worth copying. This is where it has to begin, you know—each man looking after his own attitudes and his own behavior, judging others is a secondary thing. Right now, one of our largest problems is that we judge other men according to what they do to us. It is high time that we started changing our thinking—we must judge other men according to what they do to themselves.

Dignity

The city is quiet today. Many stores, banks, and offices have closed and the people have disappeared. Right now New York is lovely, left alone to think itself out. The silence in the streets, the absence of so many taxicabs, even perhaps fewer pigeons around the place today. I can see one on a window ledge across the way from my apartment building. He has a twig in his mouth, carefully working it into a nest, I guess. A pigeon doing a little personal work before the city gets busy again.

It will be quiet for three days now. The city can rest, sleep, awake, and be ready for Monday to come. If only when they (the people) return, they would give this place a chance to continue to rest, sleep, and arise—some peaceful time in which to renew itself once in a while. It's a pretty city now, with promises of life and hope. Can we give it a chance?

Today, looking around, I could live here forever. Monday, we'll see how I feel. The city has pride. Not false pride, but the real thing—a certain dignity. Where is ours?

Where Credit Is Due

When God gives something, he really gives it fully without any question marks attached. To some performers, he has given talent to the point of genius. Art Tatum, for example, was an unbelievable pianist. When he died, his close friends literally buried his piano with him. Yet I have heard people say, "Oh, I could have written what he did." I always think, "How lovely, sweetheart, then write it. But then who is going to play it the way he did?"

You see, some of the really topflight geniuses have never been given the credit they deserved. I think that Ella Fitzgerald is the greatest singer in the world. She is well respected, but I think that she has more talent and more influence on our music than anyone realizes. She has an instrumental voice, smooth as velvet. I always thought of Dinah Washington as a singer with almost perfect diction, a very rare gift. She was never fully recognized for what she had. In some circles, genius makes its own way.

I remember years ago, sitting in a certain theater and listening to a young lady singing. Behind her, a young piano player was really swinging. All at once the audience seemed to realize the nip of sheer joy at seeing a genius. At about the same time, the spotlight man, as if by instinct alone, moved off the singer and onto this fantastic piano player. Every ounce of attention was riveted on the accompanist.

The intensity of his playing was larger than life. He was tiny in stature, but larger than anything around him, and he never looked up. The lady singer was furious because her act was completely shot to hell. She left the stage after that number and fired him for good.

Well, he had come all the way from Pittsburgh, and now he was fired. I learned that he couldn't read music, but I still felt that he played one powerful piano. I had a little thing going at Town Hall one night, and I asked this young man to accompany me. He agreed. At one point in the performance, I set him up for a solo. With a noble gesture of my hands, I stepped aside and said, "Now listen to this." The young man really took off. As he played, I prayed to myself, "Lord, don't let them forget me during his last eight bars, and just let me stay close to this piano."

The audience seemed to know that they were seeing the birth of something. In fact, they were right, because the young man's career continued to grow. Now he is recognized as one of the jazz greats, the author of "Misty," with a style all his own. I shall always think of him as the man who moved a spotlight without touching it—Mr. Erroll Garner.

All There

When I went to see *Coco*, with Katharine Hepburn, it was all there. At one moment in the play there are tears running down her face. Those tears came out and hit me like a light. Some performers, it seems, can just set you up. It is hard to describe what that genius is, but I think that I've heard someone say that when a genius walks on the stage, one doesn't know whether the roof is going to fall or the stage will melt—but one knows something is definitely going to happen. There are people who have this power emanating from them, even as they walk into a room. Recently, I picked up a magazine. Garbo's face was on the cover. I realized that there was no need for me to read the story. It was all there in her face, all there.

Boy Pride

Like a little boy he said, "Guess what I'm doing—I've put some bread in milk to make it soft and I'm feeding her." He was speaking about his mother who was old and ill.

"Does she know you?"

"No—but can you imagine me doing this?"

Sure I could. Yeh, I could imagine that about him. I could see him doing it, but I couldn't think of anybody else who would be able to imagine it.

I knew his warm qualities, the ones he hated to show. I knew them because I had seen these qualities in short flashes of personal beauty. This last was the prettiest flash of all—his announcement of what he was doing. It was cute because he was obviously so terribly proud of himself for being himself.

The Game Well Played

The Mets were meeting the Orioles in the last game of the World Series. Those are my boys, the Mets. I had had good ESP radiations about them all season long, even when they were only one ahead of last place. Now they were taking on the Orioles. I stepped into the bullpen. Jerry Koosman was getting ready to exercise his arm a bit. He walked over to me and said, "Pearl, there's only two people I wanted to see today—you and the man from *Sports Illustrated*." I don't know yet why he was after that guy, but whoever he is, he can't be the Mets fan I am. After we shook hands, suddenly the strangest thing happened. I saw big number eights all over him. Not wanting to frighten him I said, "Maybe it means you're going to get eighty thousand dollars next year." Well, the rest is history.

I sang "The Star-Spangled Banner" and went to my seat to start rooting. The Orioles went ahead, and the crowd got quiet. I took over my whole section of the ball park, yelling at those people, "If you've got faith in them, what are you so quiet about? Either you believe or you don't." The cheers started again, and the Mets went on to victory.

The crowd poured out onto the field and clods of turf were thrown sky-high. The field was wrecked and bedlam reigned. I went into the clubhouse, and finally into the dressing room. I'm not sure, but I think that Mrs. Payson, the owner, Joannie Hodges, the manager's wife, and I were the first three women to be in there. The champagne was poured over everyone. The men went wild. The TV cameras came in and everyone was kissing one another. Everyone was in love with victory!

The calmest person of all was the man who led them to victory. A giant of the game, Gil Hodges. He is a man who knows his men, his business, and is always desirous of perfection. Some have criticized Gil for wanting his way a bit too much. All I can say is if any of his players do as well in baseball as their manager, then they can criticize. Gil has found the secret. He is not seeking fame for himself. He simply likes to see the game played well.

No Closing

It was time to leave. I had done more performances in *Dolly* than any other leading lady. A beautiful chapter at the St. James Theatre was coming to an end. The show was going to hit the road.

Once on the road, I got a call from Jack, our general manager. "It's so sad and lonely here without your company. It's raining today. You know, Pearl, even the sky is crying." Broadway may be in shock when they read that this tough sledge hammer, Jack, made that beautiful statement. We were a lively company in New York, and Lord knows we had a bit of color there. After we left, everything turned pale. I used to enjoy being there in the afternoons to watch our group come in to the St. James. The young ones with their sensational getups of the times. It was quite a sight. Hell could be raised and lowered, but something warm will remain there on that stage. When we left, you bet your fanny the sky cried. And loneliness set in on all of us. We were never to return. *Dolly* continued, but the ghosts of our company of '68, '69, and '70 walk there still. For them, that show will never close.

They Should Have Seen Me

On April 10, 1970, I was called on to do an evening at the White House for President and Mrs. Nixon and their guests, Chancellor Willy Brandt and his wife. They found me in Detroit playing *Dolly*. After the Friday performance, I left for Washington. Few things have ever excited me more as a performer than playing the White House.

My dear friend Mrs. Perle Mesta heard that I was on my way to Washington. Although she was in California, she wanted me to stay at her apartment with Edna, her long-time devoted friend and housekeeper. As I went in there, I found myself thinking back to the beginning of my career. Both Mama and Papa crossed my mind. If only they could have been there. "Look, parents, I'm staying at the Ambassador's house, from here I'm going to the Big House. Hot dog!" Mama was always so proud of us. I found it going over and over in my head, "Guess what, Mama! I'm going to see the President tonight."

Mrs. Mesta came all the way back from California early to oversee my appearance at the White House. Also, as the time was approaching, Mr. Merrick called. He had heard that I was about to appear at the White House, and he wanted to wish me well.

Mrs. Mesta treated me like I was her daughter. I put on my long black dress with a train about three feet long and ostrich feathers about two feet deep. I was really ragged out. I had also brought a black sequined pants suit. I said, "I think I'll sing in this." Mrs. Mesta said, "Oh no, keep the dress on." I pranced out into her Louis XV dining room, proud as a peacock. Someone noticed a little bit of flesh coloring under the dress at the shoulder. "Edna, get a needle and thread," Mrs. Mesta called. Together, they sewed me in a bit tighter. I gave three or four more turns and then I was all set.

I said, "Roz, take the pants suit anyhow." I could see myself trying to dance and move around with those dern feathers. I was afraid I would fall flat on my face, or worse.

It seemed like a very long time I waited for the man to pick me up. The strain began to show on me. I could have sworn those feathers were ruffling. They were supposed to get me at 7:30. At ten minutes before eight, I had to leave the apartment, because I knew something was wrong. Had they forgotten? I figured, "What the hell, I'll walk over there. I'm not about to waste this fancy getup." As I reached the front door of the building, a man came dashing around the hall. He had been looking for me on the other side of the building. We were late, so he whisked me away to the White House. Within a few short minutes, I was entering with two dashing marines as escorts. They walked me to my place in the receiving line. My feet, incidentally, were killing me the whole time. The man behind me kept stepping on those doggone feathers. They were coming off. The cotton-picking things were everywhere.

Now I saw them. There they were. The President and Mrs. Nixon, Chancellor and Mrs. Brandt. The President spoke. "How are you—you can sing what you want tonight. You sang 'Bill Bailey' for me in '56." (That had been my first visit to the White House, at the invitation of President Eisenhower.)

Eventually, we were ushered into the state dining room. What a table it was, set with a gold service. I visited with Mr. Ehrlichman, Presidential Assistant on Domestic Affairs, and General Lucius Clay. There were speeches and toasts and Chancellor Brandt made a wonderful talk. It was time for the entertainment.

Oh, Mama, here I go.

By now I had arranged that train on my dress about fifty times, and I thought, "Don't try working in that thing, Pearl, you'll be finished." I found darling Penny Adams of the White House staff, and we went into an office so I could change into the pants suit. Okay, it was time. I noticed the quivering that always comes when I perform anywhere at all. At least I was comfortable in my clothes.

The program was a huge success. Those ninety-six people cheered like a thousand. I did a number with the wonderful Sergeant Ben Sanger, the wonderful Fiddling Marine. We had three good musicians behind us all evening. Bernie, Milt, and Mousie. Just enough sound for the East Room. At the finale, the President jumped up on the stage and gave me his chair so that I could climb up onto the piano. He did it in a very appropriate, spontaneous way. I have found Mr. Nixon to be a man of good humor and excellent timing. I just completely disagree with those people who claim that he is humorless. Anyway, the audience loved his gesture and they roared. I remarked to the Chancellor, "See how much fun we have over here. You must come over more often. Maybe when you get a chance, you'll autograph my program." The Chancellor is no slouch when it comes to wit either. After that number, someone handed me a program at the edge of the stage. Brandt had signed a card, "The Chancellor."

At the end of the performance, instead of bowing finally, I picked up Mr. Nixon's chair near the piano and left with it. As an encore, I came back and took out the geraniums that were around the stage, and people screamed. I did it as a joke, because during the show I had remarked on the probable value of the chair and the geraniums and had said that I had a convenient spot for both. Looking back over my shoulder, I spotted the President behind me with the other pot of flowers, laughing like he was having the best time of his life. We put everything down, and he took my hand and led me back into the room. Chancellor Brandt, his wife, and Mrs. Nixon joined us on stage. I sang "Hello, Dolly!" again and joined together the hands of President Nixon and Chancellor Brandt as a gesture of love. Mama, your baby girl was smack in the middle.

All the dignitaries began to come to the stage to shake hands—Senator Goldwater, Vice President Agnew, Secretary Laird, and many others. At last, a quiet voice spoke to me. "The President would like for you to come upstairs." I didn't realize at that time how rare this was. Very few people are ever invited to the second floor by any President. That's private living quarters. I got into an elevator, and when I stepped out, there they were waiting for me. (Mama, Papa, sisters, and brothers, can you believe this? I'm upstairs in the White House.)

They showed me all the rooms and explained everyone. I saw the mantel that Lincoln leaned on to sign the Emancipation Proclamation. I stood in Eisenhower's favorite room, and in the small room where President Nixon works late at night, piano albums lying around. As we walked down the hall, he asked, "Pearl, what are you going to do with that chair?" I said, "What chair, Mr. President?"

"I'm giving you that chair. It's fragile, but it's yours." My knees almost buckled. I had never heard of such a thing. I'm not sure, but I think it was one of the few times that furniture has been given out of the White House.

Mr. Nixon said, "You're one of the fastest ad-libbers I ever heard. You've really got a brain."

"And I use it too, Mr. President," was my reply.

We walked down the hall toward the elevator. Mrs.

Nixon (frail and lovely) walked alongside her husband, smiling but saying little. What a strong woman.

I said, "I wish Mama could have seen this."

Mr. Nixon said, "She did, Pearl." Then he repeated it with great warmth.

Unto Myself

I am naked unto myself.
I cannot, must not, hide from man
or me.
I search the corners of my heart for what is good.
An aim.
A corner for the right words,
A corner for right attitude,
A corner for my fellow man,
And one for gratitude.
Attitude sets up the search—
I want to be a part of life.
At the end is gratitude—
The sweetness of fulfillment.

Better in God's time . . .

Wishing Gone

At some point in a young life
It pays to spend time wishing—
I knew those days.

Wishing was that wanting to achieve,
So important in my youth—

These days I do not wish
So much for things to happen.
I've achieved so much,
Much more than I once
Wished for.

Lately, I've observed that,
Wishing gone, I've changed
To hope.

In Good Time

When I was young and disappointed I remember thinking,
"But I could do that part. Why should it go to someone
else? My heart is broken. I know it's because she's prettier,

maybe, but not more talented. Maybe there's a bit of romance there with the casting director. That's got to be it. Or maybe it's prejudice. If these are the breaks, I may as well give up. They'll never give me a chance."

In time, life has turned about. Here it is, fame and fortune, the fawning and pawing. With it, I have found laughter and understanding. Good Lord, the hours are long. Sit for some pictures. No time to eat. Forget about vacation. An extra rehearsal. Those with larger parts work a little longer. Come in early to give my opinion on this, on that, etc.

I'm glad now that I didn't make it when I thought best. Better to make it in God's time than in mine, because now, a little older, a little more mature, I can cope with it, almost.

Warmlight

Walking in a field, I turned around
In time to see, across the shaded ground
An edge of yellow warmlight in pursuit.
It slipped beneath, around me without sound—
A farewell present from a restless cloud.

In my idle time out from the fray
The field and sun came close to me to say
That rushing to succeed, as was my right,
To get ahead, and then ahead again, I had
    outrun my light.

Competition

My son Tony came home and said that some of the children were ahead of him because the teacher was not giving him all the attention he thought he deserved. He was doubly upset I think because on that same day he had lost in athletics. Tony is not the best loser in the world. What should I say?

For a while I didn't say anything. Then finally, "Well, what is it? Is it the anger that you did not beat the other fellow? Did you want to be ahead of him as a competitor? Or as an envious person? Was the act of outdoing someone more important than the act of performing well yourself?"

He couldn't answer.

I wasn't sure he understood the difference. I said, "Tony, if you would win to outdo your fellow man, how would this enrich your sense of values? You have to ask yourself at the same time how important achievement is for itself. Then try to balance the scales. Just to be in competition with a man in order to get ahead of him or to gloat over your victory later on is vain. This should not be the most important issue in your life. Why don't you just walk? Literally do it all with ease and love. Because the shadow before and after is yours."

Ambition

Children, you must remember something. A man without ambition is dead. A man with ambition but no love is dead. A man with ambition and love for his blessings here on earth is ever so alive. Having been alive, it won't be hard in the end to lie down and rest.

That Fellow Hope

Every day I hear around me,
"Never give up hope,"
The cry of all mankind, it seems
For money, fame, and friends.
But something's missing in the wish
That doesn't join that fellow hope
With faith and charity (for which read love)
Without which you'll be left with just—
I hope, I hope, I hope.

Talent Rights

Should the carpenter put on
The king's red robes,.
And also vice versa?
Why sure, by God they're equal!

But if the nailer
Cannot reach to rule—
And if the king
Can't drive a nail,
Then high and low
Both king and carpenter
Must fail.

Progress

I sat on the beach looking at the mountains and thought: the power of what exists naturally in this world needs no magnifying by man. Even man's thoughts and dreams can never reach to conceive what is already here. Surely men have sat and dreamed of hills, but where is the man who has dreamed of hills without first seeing one?

No, in the name of progress, man dreams of lesser things. Take the telephone, for example. Man dreamed up this gadget in order to save some time or save his legs. He wanted to be able to say what was on his mind immediately, no matter where the other fellow was. I'm not so sure even that was a good idea. Sometimes I think it would have been better if man had never touched those wires. When man is about to speak, it's usually better if he spends a few quiet moments considering what he is going to say, and whether he really wants to say it at all.

Everything has its value if it is used properly. It just seems to me that man has a strange habit of fulfilling his dreams with things that later become causes of destruction. There aren't any real shortcuts.

The Years

The years pass
We grow—
Upward,
Downward,
Into eternity,
Into nowhere.

As the years pass
We go.

Streisand

Frank Sinatra is known as "The Chairman," and they call
Ella "The One and Only." And not too many years ago, a
very young lady came out of the blue and was tagged
"Super Star." I know that for a very young performer this
kind of super celebrity status can cause problems. The reputation becomes larger than life and people expect too
much. I learned something about this recently by watching
Barbra Streisand.

The first time I met her, she was like a little girl. She had
come to see *Dolly* (this was before the film was made) with
Elliot Gould, a doll himself. They came to my dressing
room after the performance and Barbra stood shyly.

The next time we met was at the International Hotel in
Vegas, much later. The occasion was her first nightclub
stint after TV and films, concerts, etc. By this time, she was
a huge lady in show business, with a reputation that probably no one could live up to. After her show, we went downstairs to her dressing room and had some pictures made.
Then we went into one of the rooms in the back. Barbra sat
on the floor, still in her gown. I sat on the bed (that's rare
for me, because Mama never let us sit on the bed).

Barbra had opened a couple of days before, and her re-
views had been a disappointment to her. Though the place
had been jammed, the newspaper people hadn't been particularly kind in their comments the next morning. She had

changed a song or two, and business was great, but there was a disappointment.

"Pearl, what do they want?" (A tiny voice.)

"Barbra, they expect you to be Super Woman. From all they've heard about you, they expected that when the curtain went up, you'd be standing there with diamonds hanging from your nose, and a crown four feet high standing on your head. Instead, they found a simple girl in a simple chiffon dress. And what she did was sing—no handsprings, no tightrope walking."

Really what I saw sitting there on the floor was a frightened little girl-woman, very hurt for the "love-of-people" sake. It had happened to her. Maybe she had been told just once too often how stupendous she was. You have to expect that something of that is going to stick. They had smacked her in the face with "Super Star," and she had almost come to think that nothing could go wrong. I thought to myself, Barbra, you're stuck, and you're welcome to it. Try not to be frightened, honey. If you think you're frightened, you should see the people behind the scenes in your organization. They don't run into your kind of talent and courage often. Lots of them know that if you don't last, they won't either. That frightens them, baby. For your sake and theirs, try to keep them from pushing you up on the clouds. I have always felt that the earth is my home, and I know that it is yours too.

Frankly, if I had been Barbra, coming back to nightclubs from TV and movies, I would have first taken a gig on a talk show or at a hotel in the Catskills like Grossinger's or the Concord. Nightclubs call for a different pacing. You can lose it in TV and movies. And nobody should put down these places in the Catskills. Really, they are more than just a place to get ready for nightclubs elsewhere. Some of these places pay more for one day than many others do for a week. They have a fine clientele and an audience that knows exactly what's going on. You can feel your pacing coming back, that sense of what's right or wrong with your program. You season yourself a bit and get ready.

In TV and movies, the camera reaches out and carries your image to millions. They can do things to that film or tape to help you come across. On a nightclub stage, it's like working alone in vaudeville, another thing entirely. You have to touch the people directly. They must feel you and you must feel them in that room.

I had occasion to see Barbra again later, on the stage at the Riviera. Her charm and talent "all hung out" (as the kids say). She was magnificent, at ease with life.

How To Be Tired

There are many ways to be tired, but some people never realize the difference. When you are physically and mentally tired in a negative way, that is a warning. You should rest. When you are beautifully tired, you should admit it and be thankful for the feeling. It comes when you've had a sense of accomplishment, hard work that paid off in satisfaction. When a man is beautifully tired and knows only that he is weary, he is making his own sadness. When happiness comes, he doesn't know it, but habitually calls it something else.

The Heart Machine

When you're in intensive care, as most people know, it's doctors and nurses all around the clock. Your family, and sometimes a close friend, may be allowed a five-minute visit. Many of the people who come to visit are almost sure that their loved one will not come out alive.

In Dallas, Texas, on May 12, 1970, I was lying in intensive care. I had collapsed the day before and was unable to go on the stage for the performance of *Dolly*. Through a little window, I could see the nurse on duty. They constantly watched that heart machine, because if that stops, you have. Once in a while, a patient's moving around in bed will disturb a disc, one of those metal things they put on your body to read your heart. When that happens, an alarm goes off and doctors and nurses do a hundred-yard dash to see if you're with it or without it.

As I lay there, a man, not a relative, walked in and sat in the chair over in the corner. He sat dejectedly, looking at me. Mournfully he said, "Miss Bailey, I hate to see you lying there." I had a bottle with a needle sticking in my hand and discs stuck on my body. Overhead, the heart machine was blipping away. I had watched that thing trace my heartbeat for so long that I felt woozy-eyed. I didn't understand exactly what it meant, but I had been watching it just the same. You do that. I said something ordinary like, "Well, I don't much like being here either."

He said, "You know, they turned away (X amount of) dollars last night."

That really struck me. Pretty funny, I thought, with me lying here in intensive care. I remained quiet.

He continued, "Those doctors of yours are just alarmists."

"Oh?"

"Yeh, I've been sitting out there for two hours watching that machine of yours. It's steady. Those lines are going across the same way every time."

I said, "Thanks a lot, dear. I too have been watching, sedation and all. I see the lines going across the same way every time, but did you stop to notice how long it takes that line to get from one side to the other?"

What's in a Name?

In the Americana Hotel in New York the nightclub room is called the Royal Box. It is a good room for performers, and I was glad to get myself booked in there. Before the opening, as I was rehearsing with the musicians I kidded around with them the way I always do. We had some laughs about a little girl from Newport News who finally was about to make her appearance in a Royal Box. There were some good laughs.

On my opening night, a huge crowd showed up. I honestly felt ready for it. I walked out to the applause, "Hi, folks! I know I'm going to have a ball here," and I named the room. There was an uproar of laughter that surprised me a bit. I could just tell it was going to be a terrific evening. A few minutes later, I again referred to the name of the place, and I got that same roar from the crowd. "My, my," I thought, "it's really a good gimmick to do this. I'm getting them with it."

From time to time, I would notice one of the musicians trying to get my attention. Two or three times I shot him a glance, and each time he was watching me very carefully.

Finally I once again expressed my love of "working at the Queen's Box." As the crowd went crazy again, this musician beckoned me to come over. Then he whispered in my ear. Good Lord! It finally hit me.

Opening Day

I remember the first day I arrived at my offices in the Hollywood Palace. It was the beginning of the Pearl Bailey weekly show for ABC. There it was. The desks were all set up. My immediate staff, some of whom had been with me for years, were standing around wondering where to begin —Jeannie, Dodi, Barry, DeeDee, E.B., and Laverne, ready to work. I felt that we had to talk for a few minutes, this being our first meeting, about how to go about doing business with each other and remaining friends. All these people were so eager and hopeful, and, I sensed, a bit frightened too. This was something big and they knew it.

Jeannie said, "Did you see the front door when you came in? It's got the name all printed on."

We went out and looked it over again, all of us. We just stood there smiling. It began to sink in on us though that we really had our work cut out for us. Technicians and the production staff were busy all over the Palace downstairs. So it starts.

I said, "Well, it can happen. Do we tear up the ratings, folks, and shake up TV land? Do we take a shot right at the top?"

Somebody answered, "Lady, we're going to do our best to see you do just that."

I said, "Friends, all I can deliver is what God gave me,

and that's about all you can do too. This thing has got to be governed by God. Therefore, relax. No uptightness. All love—and deliver. There's much to be done. Let's do it and talk about it later."

How To Live With Success

Terry Gibbs said to me, "Pearl, if I could only have one good taste of the success you have had in show business, then I think I would be satisfied. You can't even realize how big you really are in this business." And he went on to sing of my accomplishments, claiming that I take many things for granted. I started by trying to explain to him something about the immense love and energy that must come from God. The more I talked, it seemed, the less he understood what I meant.

The next morning, I awoke thinking of this conversation and it dawned on me what I should have said to him. "Let me give you more to hope for and less to want. If and when, and in whatever way, you may find a taste of success, you will have to be prepared to handle this great gift. Handling even a single success—the use of talent, the sharing, the holding on, the giving out and pulling in, requires special preparation. At this stage you should be hoping that if God favors you, you will maintain your sense of values—your sense of gratitude.

Loves that choke the love
that satisfies . . .

Rambling Thoughts

Whatever happened to the me inside? I was and am human. I go my way as I like, and only as I like. I do as I please. I love when I want to, or leave it alone when it gets in my way. What has happened? Did I stumble over myself? What is this nagging? Forget it. It's just a headache, perhaps a bit of depression. It's the rain.

My family is disrupted—wait! Was that a friend of his that passed? Should I ask about him? Why should I? This will pass. Still, it wouldn't hurt to inquire. It's proper and expected of one in my position. But suppose this guy tells him I was asking? He mustn't think that I am concerned, that I really care. So pass that. Back to my old self. Who needs this? Where could it lead me anyhow?

The phone! Get it! Oh no you don't! If it's him, the terror will come back. Could be an important call, not him. After all, he did not speak to me for days. So answer! Oh Lord, it's stopped. Was it? It is raining.

What a sight we must have made. We stood on a corner waiting for a cab. Oh yes, we could have stood there forever. No rain then. Only sunshine.

Gosh I'm hungry. I must be mad to let my mind wander so. I'll find the closest place. I'm starved. Think I'll take a book with me because I don't want to talk to anyone. A table in the far corner, please, alone. No, nobody is going to join me. Silly man. Do I look like I want to be bothered. I guess I'll have . . . Now what the hell is that he always ordered and let me taste? The waiter would know. I won't ask. I just don't want to say his name to the waiter. I just ask casually, "Waiter, what was that dish . . . ?"

"Yes, Miss Bailey, very good."

Big mouth! He didn't even give me a chance to finish. Named the dish and spoke his name. I'll order something else. I can't read after all.

Who's the waiter smiling at behind the post? He motions to my table. My God, it's him, yes, coming to my table. The waiter presumes too much. Who asked him anyway? I said I wanted to be alone, didn't I? There's nothing to do but be polite.

"Care to join me?"

"Oh! I don't mind at all."

He'll order that same dish we had before. I'll just snack as usual. Something blah.

"Have a drink? You look fine."

Ah ha! He is nervous—smoking. Blushing a little—a little shy. I excite him. He does like me still. What was I worried about? He still wants me badly. Suffer, my friend. My friend, suffer.

Now my insides are still. The tightness is gone, and I am all warm again. He excites me too. I love him still. I need him to love me. I hate suffering.

My Insides Out

Whenever I felt myself going too far, I steeled myself against it—afraid to express too much, to feel too strongly. If I would show myself, my inner self would disappear. Someone might gain an insight into my personality, so long kept secret. What was mine was mine.

Opening a gift, I'd want to be alone—like a little child at Christmas, greedy from never having had enough. I would relish the possession. The thought that someone had given me something all my own. "Lock all the doors and windows so it can't escape. Nobody must touch it!" I withdrew.

Even a letter—"It's mine. The paper and the words on the paper are mine. Lord, he does care!"

Laughter. My front was gone, my insides out.

It is a fear one finds usually in a person who is bigger than he knows he is, yet more shallow than he wants to be known to be.

The Vines

Married people can get so caught up in their separate careers that they wind up in divorce or else continue to get more miserable each day. It is a kind of trap that awaits anyone who gets too deeply into his own bag.

Vines are useful in many ways. They can be decorative, comforting, beautiful. Still, you have to watch them or they will creep across the lawn and cover the house while you are inside and not looking out. They can cover your windows of life. For a very long time, Louie and I forgot to prune the vines. We weren't even aware of them. We withdrew into our lives, reclusive.

We were two performers with two wonderful children. I think I noticed the danger first when our children began to take on some of our habits. Also, I think I began to notice it because I was the one who had to be away from home. I began to sit and enjoy other human beings, something I hadn't done sincerely for a long time. Louie, being a warmer personality in some ways than I am, always embraces people a bit more. I am tempted to draw inside.

I found my clue in reaching out to E.B., Peetney, Dodi, and a few others. We had to learn to find enjoyment in New York during *Dolly*. We alternated between the Manhattan Grill, Act 4, and fancy-pancy Sardi's (on the nights when we felt like living high-on-the-hog). We found ways to laugh. Lots of times at nothing. Perhaps because we all were fighting loneliness. Anyway, in the midst of that, the vines fell away from me. I cut them with imaginary scissors. There were people out there, and after fifteen years I was really seeing them and appreciating them. I was emerging.

For single people, the vines aren't apt to grow across the windows. I never went out very much, even before I met Louie. I am basically a homebody. I wasn't one for socializing, gallivanting, and going crazy socially. Still, as I began to emerge from this darkness, I realized that fifteen years before we had been able to have beautiful times. There was no reason to have shut that off.

Louie was having difficulty too. Living in California, missing me, he had imbedded himself in music only. The vines grew over our house. Engrossed in his music, he never even pruned the vines. Inside, he felt safe, protected, consumed in his musical work. As he saw it, I was out where humanity was, and therefore, unsmothered. He wasn't worried about his own turning inward.

Maybe he was slow to realize what was happening because he has such concentration. Many a time I have walked into his office at the house to find him working in almost complete darkness. He would be writing music on pages he could hardly see.

The point is that as engrossed as we may get in our professions, we must take time occasionally to draw back for perspective.

Vancouver

I used to sit by the window every day and sew.
Louie was writing music
And DeeDee was being DeeDee.
The courthouse was across the street from our hotel.
From an angle I could read the news of the day
On the *Sun* Paper Building.
Between stitches I did a bit of mail from the pile
On the huge table in front of me—peeping now and
    then at Louie in his private world of music.
I watched people walking in the rain
(It rained practically every day there
Every hour
On the hour
Yet no one seemed to care.)
It fascinated me to see
The real don't-care-if-it-rains attitude
Of the people—
The beauty was that everyone seemed to be

Perfectly content
To let God have his privileges
Without mumbling or grumbling.

Need for a Fence

When I was working for Rose Calderone in Pittsburgh, I
lived in New Stanton at the Holiday Inn. Chuck King and
the entire family got me to calling it home. Up the road were
some stores where I did my shopping. Driving back from
there one day, I did a double take. What the heck was I
looking at! It was a man standing on the hillside by the
trees exposing himself. I was incensed! It was two-thirty or
a quarter to three. Up the road, I could see little girls in
uniforms (Catholic-school girls) on their way home. I
know that people who do things like that are sick. But all I
could think about was those little girls (like mine) who
soon would be passing by.

I turned the car around and headed back to the village
where the market was. I knew there was a police station
there. I went in fuming. The man said, "Can I help you,
lady?" Can you get this picture—Pearlie in her old slacks,
old hat, groceries on her arm, fuming like anything? "You
gentlemen will have to do something about this disaster up
the road." That was my opening line. They were cool. One
said, "Oh, you're the one that sings." I said, "Never mind
the singing. There's a man up there with his (and before I
realized what was coming out, I had said it)—bare ass
showing and waving his business at little children."

The whole police station broke up. The cop said,
"There's a home up there. Lots of old men in the place, and

we do get lots of complaints." I said, "Have you? Then why the hell haven't you put up a wooden fence or something? Why hasn't something been done? The usual procedure, I guess—after the cow is out of the barn?" Oh, I raised some hell.

I speak very deeply about this. Nothing in the world could be more frightening to a little girl than to get mixed up in something like that. I knew one who had to be taken down to a detention home to see a doctor for an examination. She was young, not knowing why she was being examined, hardly knowing what her organs were. It stays and stays, that experience. Things like that show why today so many men and women, even as they grow older, think of sex as the ugliest thing in the whole world. That can ruin a marriage too.

Many people who are called frigid really are frightened. It takes a lot to help them find their warmth again.

When I was little, we lived in an apartment building in Washington, D.C. This nice, sweet man, a pullman porter, or something other than a laborer, had an apartment on the corner of the ground floor. He was warm, friendly, well respected, elderly, a real Santa Claus. All the young kids wanted to go to the store for Mr. X when he needed anything. He gave them nickels and dimes, not pennies, and that was a fortune. He seemed to love us so much, such a gentle man. We loved to go into his apartment to look at pretty things. Usually, he let the little girls do his errands for him.

All at once, something about him seemed repulsive to me. While I was looking at the beautiful ornaments in his apartment, he would sometimes rub my hair. I didn't actually suspect that it was a sexual thing. How could I?

Later on, the older people in the building became suspicious of some of his actions, and they were confirmed. The man wasn't run out of the building, but the children were told to stay completely away from him. He started going to the store for himself.

Sitting with Reason

Good and bad things have depth. It's the relationship between the two that matters. I think about my earlier marriages. It seems to me now that sometimes I felt the good things about a husband, and sometimes I seemed to feel only the bad things. I couldn't keep the scales in balance. Really, it should have been the whole person always.

Sex, in itself, is given too much importance in most marriages. What really matters is that you look across the room and get that crazy feeling. No mattress is really necessary.

"We haven't made it for so many days and nights—do you still care?"

"Don't be silly, of course. And anyway, is that the proof you need?"

That kind of thing can lead to a real spat. There is the warmth of somebody, of their being, that is stronger than any sexual relationship could ever be.

I am talking about the satisfaction that comes in the touch of the hand or a look. Talk about the population boom —if the right touch or glance could produce babies, we would have loaded the world years ago. By now, the population would have boomed out of sight. There would be a difference, though, because all of those babies would be "love babies." Instead, today too many babies are produced by parents who lie down in hatred, filth, drunkenness, and drugs to have sexual intercourse. We are reproducing out of our agonies, and the boom is bust.

I have been through the jealousy and hurt of broken marriages. There is a huge sense of loss when you realize that you do not need and are not needed anymore. Before the end, I knew that I could live very well without my marriage. In the realization, I felt that I was becoming more somebody than before—more mature and independent.

In a lasting marriage, each person has to do good for the other in the best times and the worst. Some people make the mistake of waiting in life until they are in certain positions of success or happiness to do things for others. My hurt came mostly because my marriage partner never seemed to express his caring for me when there was a lot of happiness going. On the other hand, he seemed always to turn against me when misery could be added to misery. Now I ask myself, "Did I also add to the misery?" Yes, I suppose I did. I should have stayed happy within myself during those times, then maybe I wouldn't have seen it all as misery. But we grow with experience, thank God for that.

I find it hard to leave people or turn on them when I have something. When I have nothing left, then I can leave. I never could separate from my man when it seemed there was a chance I could hurt him, no matter how much he had already hurt me. In all kinds of situations, I could always walk away much better when I had nothing left but understanding.

Having gained perspective on a situation, I feel I can leave it. Walking with nothing but myself, I'd pick up my little knapsack of food, friends, shelter, and start back from whence I came. Like a javelin thrower measuring his steps,

I can walk forward only when I know that I am able to step back into my own footsteps. This is what it means to sit with reason. Years ago, I sat mostly with passion.

The False Doorway

In the first place, didn't we actually put ourselves together? Have we really ever been married? Did God, who would never put misery with misery, put us together? No, my friend, I picked you with lustful, sinful eyes, and you me— and into this false doorway walked hatred. We snatched at a pretentious love every now and then. And into that false doorway walked more hatred. We were both locked inside, and the room grew small. The air grew tense, and we burst. Did God do this terrible thing to the flesh and blood he created? No. We did.

Farewell

Lovely one, come closer and adore me. Touch my hand. Let me feel your warmth. Time is passing and I am aware of your need to leave. But enjoy these few moments without a word. Live only for now just once and you will feel a desire to continue this wonderful thing called life. Say a word or two of truth, of love, and it will make me feel warm.

To a Love Gone

How could it have ever happened? There was no reason I can see why you ever came near. Why did you cross the room anyway? You knew what you were doing in the beginning. Your possessive self said, "This is what I need, can use—you were mine." You found me and you pounced on me. We fell over, you on top, me on the bottom. Me on top, you on the bottom. And we rolled down the hill. Where?

Love, love, you left so abruptly. I know you are hiding in some corner, lurking, waiting, I hope, for me. But why did you run? I do not need to search, nor should you run. Stand still. Enjoy it. What is your purpose? To forget? To hold on longer? To satisfy a longing, some inner passion, an ego (a trap for whom?)? Why are you doing this? Why did you start it? What did you hope to accomplish? What are you going to do when all the emptiness closes in on you? Someday it will, you know. Don't worry too much though. Other things will open to you and all these miseries and joys will pour out and into someone. You will live it all all over again and enjoy it and rejoice, but you will never forget.

Jealousy

One you really love is not around, but with other people. There is the possibility of being jealous. You feel that he is fonder of someone else or that he understands another one better. This is pure selfishness, a kind of love that is not, in fact, genuine. Once when I was feeling jealousy, a little bird spoke to me and said, "Of course he enjoys other people too.

If he loves you, he'll come back to you anyhow." What is required is the feeling of deep deep love, the kind that wraps itself all around your insides, but does not choke you.

There are loves that choke the love that satisfies. Real love is the love that knows that whenever and wherever you meet again, it's going to be bigger than ever. That can even be the answer to death.

Doll

For years, my half sister, Doll, had not spoken to me. There was only a resentful look when we met. After Papa passed in 1966, I told Doll all my insides about her. Later, she wrote me a letter.

> Pearl, I read your book, and I have thought about what you told me—why you had to return me to the family. I've been in the hospital a lot lately. And lying there feeling many emotions, there was time to think. More understanding came to me. I am a bit closer to God.

She spoke of many things, without complaining or hurting anyone. She poured out the good things she had found. A really nice letter. It filled me and enriched me. "Truly," she said, "I want to be your sister."

Doll, I am and always was. I even tried to play the role of mother once. In life's turndown, many times one can become bitter. Sure, I can remember when I thought, and even maybe said to you, "I'm busy now, there's no room for another sister (half or quarter)."

That competition between us wasn't good. Some people

say, "I won, and now who needs you?" But once in a while, each of us has to diagnose himself to see whether he is sick or not. Most times I find out that after I've won and said "Ah ha!" I know better afterward. Thank God we've found out what happened and we're glad to know. We no longer misuse or confuse the issues of life.

In marriage, many folks say, as I have said, "I don't want him. I think he cheats." Jealousy between man and wife, or between sisters, can make us go insane. We say to ourselves, "Oh dear, I'm losing this, the love of my life. What will I do? How will I survive?" Yet there comes a time when people who have almost lost one another stop and say, "Did I really? Was I ever really jealous?"

A couple of times in my life, what I have thought was love actually was hurt, false feelings, and a cry for something thought lacking in my life. Later I have stopped to say, "Thank God I lost him." Looking back, I know it wasn't really love—proper respect, but not love. Doll and I have come through it. We survive with love and respect.

If Only

If only in the quiet moments
You would leave my mind.

If only my insides would not churn
At the memory of your coming and going.

If only your eyes did not express
Such devotion when you look at me.

If only my flesh would not quiver
When you touch me, ever so lightly.

If only your presence didn't frighten
And excite me at the same time.

If only, on the days when you are
Lost to me, I didn't feel
The world had either stopped
Or turned so fast
That I couldn't get off,
And wait for your tomorrow.

Then I wouldn't know
That I love you,
And you love me.

Second Beginning

Dearest one,
I love you. It has been good being without anyone but you.
We sat, we enjoyed, we found moments that I had lost. All
wavering is over. At times I could see you become frightened by the fact that it was there again—saddened by the
fact that if I left it would disappear once more. No, love, we
have found it again. More hurdles are definitely coming.
But as for me, I'm going to jump them with grace and dignity and in the knowledge that you're it. All else is a joke.
We're learning to respect each other's individuality. We

had lost that along the way. Regaining that will be our answer. Ace, Queen—Blackjack.

Back Within the Circle

One night at Lake Tahoe, I finished my act. I felt very very happy because my family was in the audience. Louie, Dee-Dee, Tony, and even some of the extended family had come in for the show. I took my last bow, and went back down the hall to the dressing room. I said to my friend, Jeannie, "I saw something different in their faces; those kids have been away all summer—away from Louie and me and away from one another." DeeDee had been in Jersey and Tony had been in Georgia. So this was a revival and a renewal of something.

Soon, the kids came to the dressing room with my niece, Doris. Doris said, "Tony, tell your mother what you said when the show was over."

He said, "Mom, I've seen you many times since I was a tiny boy. But I've never seen you better as a performer. I've never seen you look better and happier than tonight." Then he paused for a while and finally said, "You were . . . cooking." I laughed because it took him so long to get the word "cooking" out. Louie and I had been saying that word for twenty years, but I had never heard him say it. Maybe he wanted to say it earlier, but instead he used to say, "You were awfully good, Mom." Now I knew that he had grown to know how much love, energy, and everything goes into the theater. In the past when he commented on my performances, he had always been talking about that theatrical personality on the stage, not about his Mama. Now he seemed to be putting the two together. A mother, dear children, at fifty-two can really "cook" like one of you young performers —if she knows how to mix the ingredients.

Every afternoon, about three, we took a trip over to the lake, the whole family. Louie and the kids would play volleyball with lifeguards and other young people. By golly, in almost eighteen years I had never seen Louie do that. All were happy. The children, I imagined, were realizing some things. "Mom and Dad are with us. At times, we have overused their affection in playing one against the other to such an extent that we almost drew them away from each other. Yet all the while, they have worked, laughed, loved us, and remained together. We children were in the circle once, and then we moved out. Now we must move back within."

Louie and I were thinking too all the while. "We're here with you, but you must understand that this love we have for you will have to be bought at face value. We have bargained enough with you over the last few years. There is no fire sale on love, with us as parents. In this family there should be no more 'proof love.' In trying to keep proving our love for you children, we ran the risk of ceasing to give to each other. So the cup is drained. And now we start again."

I had seen their faces at ringside, and I had felt them. Their faces and their manner seemed to say, "Who are these people, this man and lady? Who is this woman who radiates love to us, the love we're seeking—the love we've had all the time? Our parents are aware of us and we too must become aware of them again as parents who did theatrical work, instead of thinking of them as theatrical robots who happen to have us as children." I remembered that once DeeDee, when she was very small, had pointed to the television set and said, "I like that lady." She didn't even seem to be aware that the lady was me, her mother. She did say that the lady's face made her think of Mama's face. She'd go over to the TV and kiss the lady on the screen and then come and kiss me. Louie and I wanted very much to be known as Mom and Dad.

We adopted both of these wonderful children. Until my autobiography, *The Raw Pearl*, was published, neither child knew about the adoptions. Many times through our little trials and tribulations with Tony, I had told him, "Someday I'm going to let you read a story." He never knew exactly what I was talking about. But I knew that at the appropriate time, he could find his values within those pages. And in reading about the adoption, he could understand just how much Louie and I care.

One day I opened *The Raw Pearl* to that chapter and handed it to him. He was sitting across from me so that I could really observe him without really observing. I pretended to read *The New York Times*. He finished reading the story, sensing everything. I kept on reading for a while and finally looked up.

I said, "Well, did you finish it?"

He said, "Yes."

I said, "Well, son, what do you think?"

He answered, "It's very good. I'm a very important person, aren't I? I'm somebody."

I said, "You bet you're somebody, and that's the way it should be. We'll want to tell your sister (and she is your sister by the grace of God). Let us find the time and the way to tell her, Tony. Not you alone, so that she too will be able to enjoy the beauty of it all."

He agreed.

Today

Sitting by the pool
I thought—
Louie and I,
Eighteen years,
Almost.

Time—
Peace,
Strife,
Peace.
It comes around,
Doesn't it!

Today it's all
So pretty.

The Bond

We sit in the quiet of this room—
You are lost in your work, I in mine.
Each one needs for no one near or far
In the spiritual world of solitary thought.

Our soul work done, we turn around
To set our feet back on material ground.
I look into your face to see, or else to find
A strength in artful understanding, peace of mind.

We are together even when apart—
The sense of it is not that I am yours,
Much less that I think you belong to me.
Love does not possess; we reach beyond ourselves
To see that we belong to God's fraternity.

Let me smile
when the fire of humanity
starts to burn hot . . .

Love Under Pressure

On the way from Tahoe to New York, we made a stop in Vegas. There was a little delay. I didn't mind though, because Sammy Davis was on the plane. We greeted each other warmly. He had just recovered from pneumonia and was going back to work. This man is a great talent, but he works himself harder than necessary for success. As we stepped off the plane in New York, I said good-bye to Sammy and he zipped on ahead of me. I stepped into the terminal with all sorts of things in my hands—a red box filled with the handwritten pages of this book, my handbag, and an overnight case. I had a fun hat cocked on one side of my head. I was hobbling along with all these things and thinking, "Thank God I'm down." I heard the lady coming from one side, "There you are, there you are." It was practically like a physical assault. She was putting her hands on my face. Ugh! In her enthusiasm, she knocked my hat off and I dropped the book box. She was still rubbing my face as I leaned over to put down the overnight case. Who did she really think I was? Heavens, no one is that great. It was frightening.

Well, she had seen me on the plane and had planned the whole thing. She had gotten out first to prepare for the attack. It destroys me when I lose control of myself, yet things like that really shake me. Bitterly, I said, "Lady, you've knocked my hat off and you've held up the rest of the passengers, now you're rubbing my face with both hands. And that's the worst. Even tiny children resent getting pinched on the cheeks." She backed off only a little bit and I started gathering my things again.

One thing that helped to get me so angry and embarrassed was that under the hat I had just pulled up my hair and wrapped a rubber band around the ponytail. Then I had just tied a little scarf around up there. For a minute I thought she had got the scarf too. It was lucky for this lady that I put my hand up there to check. If I had found that scarf gone, and me standing there in the airport with that ponytail and red rubber band—if that had been my look for the evening—I'd have belted that lady all the way back to Vegas faster than she came in.

I started down the corridor. Would you believe she tapped me on the shoulder and said, "Miss Bailey, could I have your autograph?" Under my breath I said, "Lady, you can have anything in moderation." Of course, now my hands were full again, and my teeth and my nose and my toes and all. What was I supposed to be, an octopus? I stopped, put the things down again, signed the autograph, and put out my hand to shake hands. She gave me the darndest fish handshake I've ever had.

As I rode to my apartment, I went over the whole thing again in my mind, and it made me think of something that had happened only the night before. I started into a song when someone yelled, "Pearl, we love you." I stopped cold and felt goose bumps. I said, "I love you." Then I started to sing again, voluntarily. The stage grew quiet and it was quite dark. Only the pink head spot on me. I said to the audience, "You know what, I do feel your love. Once I didn't know how to accept it. I went around like an Indian scanning the horizon looking for love." (And I made that scanning gesture. People began to smile.) "Yes, I know we mutually love. Now I stand still, no more searching. For love is all around me. I don't even have to turn my head. At this present period in my life I'm experiencing such love and devotion as I never knew could be given to any human being in this world. Children, old people, dogs and cats, you name it, it's an overpowering sensation and must be handled with the greatest care. I have to respect this love because to take unfair advantage of it could only destroy me. It's a rare and beautiful thing in this world, where there is so much up-tight hatred and selfishness. I hope that you will rejoice with me that there also is still love."

Now maybe you understand why it destroys me so when I feel a flash of bitterness and lose control.

Mumbling to the Sweater

I stood at a counter in Saks Fifth Avenue down in Florida. I was talking with the saleslady, a salesman, and a charming young personal shopper, who was helping me make my way through the store. We were all kind of frozen because without wanting to, I had just given a séance to the lady waiting on me. I do that sometimes, just know things about people. Anyway, we were getting back to shopping matters when another woman, a customer like me, walked up and just stood there, listening. Things were a little crowded, so my personal shopper turned to her and said, "You can go by."

"I don't want to go by," she said. "Do you talk to every-body like this?"

"Like what?" we wondered. The young lady was trying

to be polite and failed to sense that the customer was angry.

The lady continued, "Why did you ask me to move on? I want to stand here." This lady was upset over nothing. She turned to the personal shopper. "What's your name, young lady?" Oh my, here goes the young shopper's job. The lady was about to report her—evil bag!

Gently I said, "Darling, she thought you wanted to get by or look in the case here and so thought maybe we were standing in your way." Lord, let that suffice, please.

"No," she said, "I'm determined to stand here and look at you." Now I felt funny shopping prices and all with someone listening to every word. Still, I had little choice. I was wearing a black cotton-knit sweater. The strange lady said, "This sweater is very pretty." She started feeling it. And remember now, I was in it.

"I think so, I enjoy it very much."

"Was it made especially for you?"

"No, I bought it on the corner near my apartment."

"Oh," she said, "you didn't knit it yourself? It looks like it's good." Boy, was I sick of her. I said, "It looks good, lady, and it is good. And I guess it must feel good too because you've been rubbing it now for at least twenty minutes."

She smiled, okayed that, kept rubbing and mumbling to the sweater. I kept shopping.

The Big Boy

I always notice something about people who travel by plane. They buy insurance and seem horribly concerned about themselves when they're getting ready to get on a plane.

Yet, few people, when they get off, stop to say, "Thank God I don't have to collect." This should give you some clue about what kind of flyer I am. Not long ago, a stewardess came up to me during a flight and asked for an autograph. Now I figure a person who works at that job should be the least offensive of all. I said no to her, and for a moment, I think she was a little stunned. She said, "Oh, then you won't sign up here?" I said, "No, dearheart, because number one, I'm interested in one thing up here—being still. I didn't get on here to do show business. This is not my domain. All I do is put the strap on and behave myself." And believe me, I do try to behave myself. I hardly go to the bathroom up there. It's a dire emergency when I do.

Later I wanted to go to Las Vegas. Louie was playing Caesar's with Tony Bennett. The new plane had come out, the big boy, the 747. Without even looking at it, I knew this was not my cup of tea. Anyway, I made my plans to get an early plane and called Lou to tell him I was coming. "Honey, you ought to rest," he said.

"Oh no, I want to get this early one so I can get there earlier."

Then he said, "But that's the big boy."

"What big boy?" I asked.

"The one that holds about three hundred and fifty."

I said, "Then that's out. I'm not going up there. It's bad enough that the wind or whatever it is holds the little ones up with ninety people, never mind three hundred."

E.B. took me to the airport. I was perfectly satisfied. I would simply get the next flight. It was a Saturday and the place was very busy. In the check-in line, an airline man spotted me and came out very graciously and said, "How are you, Miss Bailey, blah, blah, blah." He wanted me to move on past and get ready to board. Now I don't have a fear of death. I have a fear of *flying*. That's because I'm no bird. I keep thinking about how that big thing is supposed to stay up. I was about to board when E.B. said, "I think that this is the big plane after all." I was stunned. "What big plane?"

"The big boy, the 747."

"It can't be." As I was standing there petrified, not knowing what to do, some strange man came up to me and slapped me on the back. He said, "Ah, Pearl, you're going on the big one with us." I said, "Who is us? I'm not going anyplace with you, I'm going with the airline. I'm traveling alone." He didn't give up. He said, "This is the 747, aren't you thrilled?" I went back to the desk and asked the man. He said, "Yes, Miss Bailey, if you'll look around this way you can see it."

Looking through that huge plate-glass window, all I could see was part of the nose. Lordy! That nose alone was enough to be the regular plane. E.B. said, "Oh, isn't it gorgeous." Now I wanted to kill him. Because he wasn't going he could talk. He said, "Let's go over and get a closer look."

Now the strange man was there again. He slapped me on the back a second time. BAM! "Don't be afraid, Miss Bailey. I'm going to take you safely to Cuba."

I turned around and said, "But I don't want to go to Cuba. As a matter of fact, I don't think you're amusing and I'd rather not talk about it. And by the way, stop slapping me on the back. My nose bleeds." He said, "Yes, I'm going to hijack you to Cuba." This guy had to be drunk. It was nine o'clock in the morning, and my humor wasn't in top shape anyway. I thought, "Not only have I got this big nose plane to worry about, I've got this big mouth man who is teasing me about something that isn't funny in the first place." They called the flight and I found myself going aboard.

It looked exactly like I was going into the grand ballroom of the Hilton Hotel. Someone said, "Don't you want to see downstairs, Miss Bailey? There's time."

"No, I don't even want to be upstairs." Always, the minute I get on a plane, I go sit down, put my seat belt on, and hold very still. I'm a train lover, you see. I just don't understand what's the hurry. I know that the eagle is the largest of the birds, but God put him up there in the air. The airplane wasn't laid like an egg, sat on and nursed by Mama.

A young man leaned over and asked, "Would you mind terribly moving to another seat?"

"For what, dear?"

"So my sister can sit beside me." I'm completely irrational in an airplane, but I tried to stay calm. I said, "Son, I'm not being rude, but I am in here. I don't want to be in, but now that I'm strapped in, that's the way I'm going to stay. Because if I unstrap, then your sister and you and the rest of your family can have all the seats in this plane. This belt is all that's keeping me in here."

I looked through the window and saw E.B. standing in the airport. He was making broad gestures like, "Oh, isn't that grand." I was reading his lips. He said, "I'd love to go with you," and "I wish I could go." Several times I saw him pantomime, "It's gorgeous." Every time I saw him I liked him less. I wanted to trade places with him.

We sat and sat. Something had gone wrong. I knew it. Finally they announced that they couldn't close the door. I started thinking, "If you can't close the door, why don't I just get up and get off. We'll go find an airplane that can close the door." I called a stewardess and asked her about it.

She said, "Oh no, they're working on it. It's almost ready." Now that's all I needed—the thought of these guys working on something. The way I figure it, if one hinge isn't right, I could see myself with this open-air deal up there blowing around. We sat for almost forty-five minutes.

Once we got into the air, the sound didn't work on the movie and my stereo headphones did nothing. I decided to get deeply involved in writing my book. I figured that would take my mind off it. I tried but I couldn't think. Then I decided to try a whole new approach. I would unstrap myself, and I would get up and walk all around the airplane. In the center is the bathroom and the kitchen, and on the other side is another whole plane. In the back part, they sit across in six and eight rows, just like a big auditorium. Walking front to back, it seems like a half mile. Some people nodded and bowed as I went down the aisle, and a few asked for autographs. I always said, "Not here, honey, you'll have to get your autograph from the man upstairs, because here I don't write, He writes." I stopped to talk with several stewardesses and then headed back for my seat. I was keyed up but trying to play it a little bit cool.

I wish I had seen him before I started up that aisle, but I didn't. When I passed, he let me have it on the back again. The blood almost jumped out of my nose. He said, "Ah, I have you up here. Now I'm going to hijack you to Cuba." That nut again. I blew my cool. I whirled around in that airplane. You talk about temper. You would have thought I was Joe Louis in the prize ring. I wheeled around with my hands out front and said, "Mister, I don't think you're funny and I don't think your jokes are funny and I don't want to go to Cuba and I don't want to see Castro. Not now." I just about took him and the island of Cuba apart. He said, "Now, Miss Bailey, you've never seen it." When this loud mouth said "Cuba," heads turned on all sides. And there wasn't a smile as far as the eye could see.

When I got my strap around me again, I was the most miserable woman in the whole world. The Lord was talking to me, "You've lost control of yourself up here, Pearl, and you have no right." Oh, he was letting me have it. I was beginning to picture my punishment, just like a little kid. I figured, "Down I go."

Once I got my feet on the ground in L.A., I realized that it was five days from my return to New York. I called Dodi about the reservation. "Get a Beechcraft, a Piper Cub, or a healthy eagle, but no big boy."

What the Hell Is Wrong with Some People?

You can be as nice as sugar and they respond by taking advantage of you. I was in the midst of my work, peacefully writing away in my hotel room. I was in my nightgown and I had the music on. The housekeeper of the hotel came in in her nice crisp uniform and we chatted. I offered to mail any number of pictures to her or her friends. I thought that she seemed very understanding about my need for peace and quiet. I had told her, after all, that I was writing a book. A little while later she returned with all the names for the photos. We said good-bye quite pleasantly and that was it. Terrific.

As I got very deep into writing one piece for the book, I heard the rattling of keys outside the door. Then the door opened. "Who is it?" I jumped up to see.

"It's only me, the housekeeper again." Then I looked up and another lady came in with her. They both worked at the hotel, I guess, and both were now dressed in their street clothes to go home, so I hardly recognized them. Incredible. She had actually come back and brought company.

I said, "Wait, honey, what's this?"

"Oh, Miss Bailey, this is my friend. She wanted so much to meet you—"

"Thanks a lot, but I'm writing, you know. I really didn't want company." Why had she done this, knowing the condition I was in? She had accepted my kindness before and then had done this to me. It was a complete invasion of my privacy. Things raced through my mind. I knew the hotel wouldn't condone such actions. I also knew, and it made me mad, that she would not have done this sort of thing to any other guest in the hotel.

Anyway, there I was, jumping up, feeling awkward, pulling the nightgown down, brushing back hair, dropping my pen and pencil. I completely lost my thoughts and started apologizing for being like this in my own room. Eventually it all turned to disgust or anger or something.

Who in the world can account for the motives behind a thing like that? Could it have been love for me? No, I don't think so. She wanted to show off for her friend. Okay, good for her, but at what cost? Certainly she did not make any great love affair between her and me or between her friend and me.

Anyway, when she finally backed out the door and locked it, I picked up my papers, opened a fresh page, and wrote at the top, "What the hell is wrong with some people?"

Possessed

Men who suckle at the breast
Seeking another Mother
Women who feed these once born and nursed babies
One a seeker
The other a giver
Possession never stops
How can I turn loose what I held on to for thirst of life?
How can I stop the draining
Possession
Possession
You walk so tall in daylight
And suckle at night
I walk so tall in daylight
And lie drained
Possessing neither one
Ourselves
Nurse thine own breast
Drain thine own self
That is not possession
That is sacrifice
That is love
That is freedom
That is strength
At night we then lie
Strong in ourselves
Strong in each other
Not possessive
But possessed of love
The body in its freedom
Feels the silent nursing
The enjoyment of draining

Nonpossessed
Yet possessed
Complete oneness
Complete freedom
Complete Love

Gall

I was sitting outside in Vegas one day with my manager,
Stan, and Tony, my agent. It was hot as the devil, about
111° in the shade, if you could find any shade. Tony and
Stan had come from California to talk heavy business. We
went where we thought we really wouldn't be in anybody's
way. A boy and girl walked over, and we asked them to
please excuse us. When folks see others with papers spread
out, talking business, they should not interfere. They
should simply walk away and understand. Even after we
asked, they didn't go. We tried to keep talking. Finally, I
turned and said, "I'd love to talk with you now, but we're
very busy." No good. We had those brain waves going on
and interruption would have been terrible. I couldn't help it,
I stopped everything. "All right, folks, we'll stop talking.
This man has come from California. It's 111°. We're trying
to work. Now what is it?"

The girl talked on and on, telling me where they came
from, asking for an autograph, telling me a big deal about
seeing me someplace in a show. . . . The three of us sat
there looking at them. What else could we do? I wasn't
thinking so much about myself as about the people who had
come to see me from California. They had other places to
go, appointments to keep. I started to feel desperate. I had

only two eyes, two ears, and one mouth to carry on so many things at once.

Maybe it was cruel to do so (yet I didn't feel it was). These children simply hadn't caught my message. They were like babies, selfish. They were clearly unaware of just how far off the track they were.

Kidding them a little, and hoping they would get my message, I said, "Why don't you just sit down at the next table and listen. You've already interrupted our conversation and we have to go on." Do you know, they did it! I tried to smooth things over by telling a couple of jokes about a dentist playing blackjack. They were good ones, and my little friends were hysterical. Believe it, out cold, enjoying it all. I regained the spirit of the conversation with my business associates. Then, before we got started again, I turned to the kids and said, quite politely, "Now you've enjoyed the humor, and we've met each other. Would you mind terribly now, excusing yourselves so that we can get back to business, and I can resell what I had already sold before you arrived." They left.

They might have walked away, saying to themselves, wasn't that friendly of her to take time for us? Or they might have been saying, we got the brush-off. Or they might have been saying, what the hell did we do after all? We intruded, cut across a conversation, sat down, and actually listened while they tried to do business. Was that nice? I know that I would never have had the gall to do what they did.

Incidents like this make me stop to ask myself whether I have grown large enough to be what people call a "star." Stars are just going to get it no matter what they do. Before you get into it, you have to know how much you want to remain a person. If you're not very careful, it can do bad things to you. Many "stars" spend a great deal of time trying to overcome feelings of inferiority. I find there are moments when I feel far superior to others, not as a performer but as a person. Yes, many times I feel superior in the fact that I wouldn't disrespect my fellow man.

A lot of laymen seem to think that performers of the "Super Star" variety eat all this up. They expect it because of what they think of themselves. Okay, but think about this for a minute. Some people reach their height of popularity, still wanting to be known as regular guys. What they find is that when they are lifted above humanity, they are, in some ways, almost cast below it. It is a complete reversal. An inferiority complex is like being on the street and hearing everyone say, "Go inside." For me, it is almost as bad when I am inside and everybody else is asking me to come out.

Down in Florida in 1970, I was a judge in the finals of the Miss Universe contest. After one session, seven of us headed for Wolfie's Restaurant. There was a long line outside, as people waited to get in. As we stood there, some of the people noticed me and started kibbitzing. It seems to come natural to some people to kid me about my feet and so on. But I guess I ask for that by joking about them myself. Hungry as I was, thank God I had the energy to stand there and smile and be pleasant.

After a while, one man said, "Pearl, why don't you go right on in? Do they know you're out here?" (Good, stupid question.) "No sir," I said. But I thought to myself, of course they don't know I'm out here. There's no TV on the street, and had I called for reservations, I hope I would have the sense to go up and tell them so. Again he said, "Why don't you just walk right on in?" Another one of those brilliant lines.

I answered, "Why should I? When I walked up here, all

of you people were standing here waiting to get in. Why do you think I should get in before someone else?"

His answer, "Because you are a celebrity."

I said, "Immaterial. Everyone's got the same motive—we want something to eat."

I guess someone up at the front of the line informed the man in Wolfie's (a sweet thing to do, I guess). The maitre d' came out a side door and beckoned us in. I called to him, "Oh, I'll wait, sir." He wouldn't have it, bless him. I said, "Maybe some of these others will be angry if I go in."

"Never mind, Pearl. . . ." So in we went, seven strong. As I went in, I heard voices behind me. "No we won't, Pearl, we won't be angry." I was thankful to them, but my feelings still remained. "What's in a name?"

The fact remains that I sometimes feel I must close out these people who lovingly give me special privilege. There are times for concentration, and concentration is immensely important to me. I was in Philadelphia on July 1, 1970. Mr. Walter, my stepfather, had just died. I was there to settle the sale of the house. It was hot. Goodness, Walnut Street was burning. I had driven down from New York in the early morning, emotionally full with what I had to do.

When I got to Philadelphia, all I could think about was a cup of coffee and a moment to think. Down the street from the title building, I saw a coffee shop. When I entered, I felt the impact. "There she is!" I headed for a back table. Then I ordered a cup of coffee and went to the ladies' room. When I came back, looking for my coffee, the place was an uproar. The inevitable question-and-answer period began.

I asked, "Please, can't I have the coffee now? I've only got fifteen minutes." After a while, hoping it would help, I explained what my business was for the day. I guess I wanted a little sympathy, besides a cup of coffee. No luck.

"The lady in the back says she'll give you a free manicure just to meet you."

"Thanks, but I've got to go. Just a coffee please."

Three or four times she came back with the manicure offer. Now I had my coffee, but couldn't drink it, it was getting colder, and fifteen minutes had dwindled to about seven and a half. Now the manager came over. He was a nice man, and I gave him his autograph. Now I was about out of time. I told everyone that I was sad, rushed, and wanted to be alone. Again, it didn't work. When the people who work in a place bother you, it really is a drag. They leave other customers, brush people off, and then they say they love you! Suppose performers, who are also people, would stop on that stage and start talking to friends in the wings or carrying on a conversation with someone in the audience. If we would stop performing when it was our business to perform, it wouldn't be tolerated.

The manicure-asking lady came back to make the offer still again. I started to burn. "Lady, first off, I've had one manicure in my entire life. Secondly, if I ever wanted another manicure, I wouldn't want it right now—but I will take a cup of coffee." My first cup was stone cold. "Maybe I'll take a corn muffin." Two ladies walked up. Lord, I thought, here we go again. They had heard my story, and they looked very sympathetic. I explained that I wanted to talk but didn't have the time. One waitress watched all this from the side. I could tell that she had realized what a bad thing was going on, but she couldn't help. Now my second cup of coffee was getting cold. I thought, "Don't they understand death?" I was about to be late. I said, "Ladies, please excuse me. Rather than sign autographs, may I just smile at you? Or maybe you could hand me your name and address, and I'll send you a picture later on."

I was pleased to hear one of them say, smiling, "How sad for you. When do you people in the theater have any peace?" Sweet lady, she walked away. (Bless you, dear, wherever you are.) But the other one stayed. She piped up, "I really feel for you but would you mind terribly autographing something for my son. He's fifteen and wouldn't believe I have seen you." Okay, great, but she had no pencil and no paper. I borrowed the stuff. Still, I had no muffin and hadn't had one good sip of coffee. I blew. "Lady, you are something else. You stood here and shook your head, understanding my story, showing me some love in your heart, and I believed you. Now just give me the paper and pen (I signed), give this to your son. I wish right now that I could give you as much love as my handwriting expresses to your son. But I must be honest with you. My heart is not full for you now. People like you are not enjoyable. I wonder if your good friends and family get the same treatment."

She just kept that smile on her face, nauseating to me by now, and said, "I know what you mean." She walked away, still smiling as if she had just said, "Merry Christmas, Happy New Year." For just a moment, she made me feel terribly cold and tired of the human race.

Pleased To Meet You

I was at Kennedy Airport very early in the morning, sleepy. I was about to go home to California from New York. A well-dressed man said, "Excuse me, aren't you Pearl?" I said, "Yes, but I've got to wee-wee." You see the man had followed me, without knowing, I'm sure, into the ladies' room. He smiled, shook my hand, and left.

The Real Fans

A crowd can be possessive about a popular performer, and they can show that possessiveness in various ways. Sometimes they swarm over the performer, hysterically pushing each other, and sometimes fighting. They are rude, doing anything to get at what they want, which sometimes is only a touch or a glimpse of the performer. Frank Sinatra created that kind of thing at the Paramount. The Beatles, Aretha, and many of the big new record artists create the same kind of hysteria. It's unbelievable madness. Now I hear that in certain crowds, women are throwing panties onto the stage. Now you tell me the reason. I can't help but think that maybe the audience is calling attention to itself.

I've seen those who truly love stand on the fringe and wait. Often those with strongest feelings stand in silence, awe, respect. It is a different kind of possessiveness—the need to have what is real without destroying it in the process.

Who the Real Friends Are

After I left *Dolly* on the road, there were some hard feelings and misunderstanding. Some people didn't know really how serious my fatigue was. Soon after I left the show in Houston, Dodi Brooks, my secretary and friend, wrote me a letter that seemed to sum up my feelings about the whole thing.

Dearest Mama:

Since leaving you at the airport on Monday, I have been quite concerned about you. I know how poorly you have been feeling, especially lately. And of course the letters written by your doctors, and your frequent trips to the hospital are testimony to the fact that you haven't been well. I can't tell you how happy I am that you didn't go to Milwaukee. And the fact that I called today and E.B. told me you are again in the hospital only proves to me that it was the wisest thing you could have done. Not out of spite or principle or anything more than the fact that God means for you to rest. He has given you warnings in so many different ways and He means for you to heed them. As long as you defy Him and try to go on, He will keep warning you. He knows you will have to listen to Him one of these times. Without going into detail, there would be many people sorry about the show from many standpoints. But damn, these people seem to be primarily the people who are your friends for more than reason. Sure, business people must protect their interests. And I guess if most of them would have to choose between their friends and their business interests, they would choose the latter. Can't blame them for that, I guess. But then you must always remember Louie, the children, and others of us who love you for you. And not for talent, success, or any of those other things. Like you often have said, if you suddenly went blind, who would be there but Louie, etc. I'm not putting anybody down, I hope you know and believe that, because thank God for some of the friends you made during the last couple of years. But I can't forget what Barbara and Art said at dinner Saturday night when talking. Some people will make you die before they allow you to know they are the least bit human. I don't feel that at this stage of your life and career you need to do this for anyone. I don't think anyone is any less a friend to you now, regardless of what they might say or do at this point. Underneath it all, they care. But I certainly think that you are proving your friendship for them in many ways. They must now understand, accept, and buy the present situation. If it all makes them less your friends, that would be sad. But you cannot afford to concern yourself with that now. You must think about Pearl and

considered sensational. I think it was actually more vulgar than most of the modern shows.

My mother-in-law, who didn't know much about the magazine, had been talking to some nut who believed everything in it. The magazine carried a smutty article about me and Louie, and my mother-in-law called me in a panic because she had heard that I had been in a raid and that Louie and I were separated, etc. Pure trash. It was soon after our marriage, and Louie was still with Duke Ellington. I did a few weeks with the show myself. I knew about the magazine article because in San Francisco, right outside our theater, this magazine was being sold. Sooner or later this magazine hit everybody. But I just couldn't believe that they had actually attacked Louie and me. For years, celebrities had seemed either afraid to sue the magazine or when they did sue, the publicity was worse than ever.

I called Miss Wright to ask her advice, because I really felt I should sue. "Pearl," she said, "don't sue them, because in doing so you will only glorify their filth. Let it go. This kind of thing dies its own death."

Several times since then, I've had occasion to exert that principle. I have refused to answer silly comments on my behavior about something, and it has worked. I found that no one really cared about the accusations. But everyone was pleased to see that I had common sense. The killer becomes his own victim.

A Strain on Love

In 1965, I spent some time in the hospital with what they called "heart strain." My doctor, whose humanness I respect very deeply, talked to me several times about my worry over the problems of others. Here was a man who himself loved every aspect of his own profession, the beautiful and the ugly alike. I guess he knew the strain involved in that.

He made me start to ask, "Should I become so much involved in the things that really involve other people?" I tried to tell myself that it wasn't I who made trouble for these other people—they got into it themselves. I couldn't stick to that reasoning. The fact is that it still breaks my heart to see a person in trouble, locked away in worry, fear, or unhappiness of any kind. I can't help but think that some ways I could help. Often Louie has said, "Honey, so and so is over twenty-one, let him take care of himself." On the other hand, my theory is if a man is going over a cliff, and I know from experience what he's in for, I've got to at least try to make him stop and think for one moment. That might be enough to save him.

I don't like to think of myself as a meddler, but as a doer. Without thinking too much about it, I often react very swiftly to the course another person is taking.

The only time that I worry about this personally is when it involves anger on my part. That does happen. I can get riled up to the point that I'm walking, completely uptight, and then I hit words hard and fast and strong. If there's an action on my part, then it's done and it's over.

That is to say, I'm not really a crier after it's done. When I do cry, it doesn't last long—give a cupful—a big sound comes out of this body. I have wept when alone. It builds up and pours out with words. I find I'm talking to myself about all I feel inside. At that point, they are not angry words, but words of hurt. I say them right out loud so that they can be heard. I can hear them and I think God can hear them too. "Lord, why did he do this? It hurts."

In moments when I feel the truest anger, I try very hard to conceal it completely. Sam Goldwyn, Sr., told me that I should always smile or I'd look angry, sick, or hurt. All my life people around me have picked that up. What the hell, my face gets tired like anybody else's. That doesn't necessarily mean anything is wrong. I feel that I have a right to meditate. It is important to do that. And when you are in meditation, you are not grinning and winking at everybody.

Looking back, I realize that I am most apt to get really angry when aggravating, nosy people draw close, and I can't keep them away at arm's length. I can sense these people coming. Like an animal, I know. I liken myself to the panther in the jungle. When he hears the enemy coming, he is ready. Sleek, he hides on a limb, or glides away into the darkness. The panther is in his domain. He knows where he is, and he is always wary. If necessary, and only then, he pounces.

Anger and hurt work a strain on love. Hurt brings tears, and anger brings hiding or violence. I try always to look alive and gay to people in public. Very often, the things that are deep in my mind have to be felt and not said.

A Childish Turn of Mind

Someone who knows my life well said he thought I had had more opportunities than most to be bitter about things—to establish a faith in hatred or scepticism. It's true, there have been some very difficult times, personal, marital, and professional. Taken altogether, they might have made some people bitter. Maybe I couldn't hold bitterness because in some respects I still have a childish turn of mind.

We were little children who went to church regularly—because our parents made us go. We acted up in church for a kind of escape. I remember that the whole idea was gorgeous to me.

When I went to church I would meet another girl my age. The children in the congregation always had to sit through the sermon. We'd wave at each other across the aisle. When the music started, the brothers and sisters were shouting and swinging. We made fun of some of the people. There were fat sisters and skinny sisters (also the sisters who hadn't, if you'll pardon the expression, washed so well). Terrible things we did! But the old folks still shouted away while the deacons and elders sat in the "Amen Corners." In the church was pomp and splendor. There were also phony things that even us kids could see.

Even then, however, I did think about religion. One thing in particular bothered me a lot. People seemed to make of God a segregationist.

"God will not like you if you are a Baptist."

"If you are a Methodist there is no hope for you with God."

Each man seemed to think that only the people of his faith were children of God.

So I had joined all the faiths by the time I was sixteen—

wow! And don't forget, my own Papa was a reverend, so we had our faith going too. Everybody tried to interpret the Bible, but nobody did it the same way. Very early, I began to wonder—when did this book, the Bible, say or mean the same thing to everybody? The fact is that when you are young, all you want to hear folks say is, "God is good and nice to know about. God will love you and you will go to Heaven if you are good."

The mind of a child searches for kindness and love— until turned into other channels.

Traps

There is a technique involved in looking at the past. The temptation is always there to try to return to something where we have found good. Sometimes, on the other hand, we are tempted to reach back for memories of the bad in order to enhance the questionable good of the present (the "good old days").

I've reached a point in my life where I somehow revert more to the good. In fact, I hardly remember the bad anymore. Oh, I have a fantastic memory all right. All my life I have been able to remember things. Lately, however, I find that I'm not telling the past the way I used to. In some cases of unpleasantness, I almost don't imagine myself as having been a part of it. Materially, I know I was. But spiritually, I think that I was not. Now, in my life, the material has been absorbed by the spiritual in me.

All of us have been caught in traps in the past. In my case, the most important ones have been the traps of lost love and miserable misunderstanding. That I have lived beyond it is enough for me. It is a trap that speaks to its victim. "Ah ha, I have your tail, your foot, and now, mister, I have your neck." Those killed in the traps cannot recall. Those who live beyond the traps can scarcely benefit from remembering them. Whether we have been trapped or set traps for others, the memories in their vividness can only bring pain, not further insight. You can only know "I did it to that rat in the trap," but the rat does not know it. He has found his peace, but where is mine? I am left with the job of emptying the traps.

And what can I do with the traps now? Shall I sell them to someone else with dirty work to do? Shall I put them in a glass cage so that I can look at them once in a while and say, "These once held someone that plagued me." Shall I save them for later in case I need them for some other rats? No. That's the point. I must get rid of them and all memories of them. If I ever reset traps, I know somehow that I shall end up stepping into them myself.

Love Power

With my heart poised in love, my emotional energy can never be drained by the challenging events of life.

The Unbelievable

I live with the Unbelievable. Every day a strength appears that my material-I could not anticipate. The Unbelievable pulls from me the manly view of life, the spiritual certainty of right. It makes me sure that the gift of understanding is the greatest gift there is. It has spoken to me of talent, God given, and even now is teaching me the doctrine of "mercy with justice." The Unbelievable speaks of love, because it knows love, it *is* love. The Unbelievable warns me of hatred, because it has seen hatred destroy the hater and the hated. It utters words of fear, knowing full the meaning without suffering the feeling. Patience and tolerance are lifeblood for the Unbelievable, and it is not in a hurry, because it is sure there is no end.

Revelation

I was in my hotel room in Vegas getting dressed. Louie was downstairs getting ready to go on with Tony Bennett. I thought I'd go down to the casino while the show was going on. The phone rang and it was Louie, who had something to tell me. While I was talking to him, a wild feeling came over me. My hand picked up a pencil and started to write. I said good-bye to Louie and hung up. Now, I didn't have my glasses on, but I was writing anyway. And a voice spoke to me. When I had come to the end, I went back to the top and wrote a title, "The Power of Loving and Living."

For about forty-five minutes I sat staring at these lines on the paper, trying to think them out, discover what they meant. One thing was clear. The message had to do with a way to live for the rest of my life with more understanding. It was telling me what I had been doing right and what I had been doing wrong in every respect—the children, my marriage, work. Still, the message was not completely clear. Here is how it read: "The more I give of myself, the less he gives of his. The less I give of myself, the more he gives of his. Are we to ask for less value, instead of a greater one? Or a greater value for a lesser one? Are we to accept more value for less? Or less value for more? Ask. Accept. What? Love."

I started listening for the little words and putting them in, gradually making more meaning. "The more I give of myself, the less he *has* to give of his." That puzzled me. If I give more, he doesn't have to give so much. Who, I asked, is he? The voice came, "He is God."

I worked on the second line. Let's see. If I give less of me, then He must give more. More love, I am sure now. If I extend less love to others and to God, then His burden is increased. The voice meant that we are brothers and sisters all. And if we share what God has given us, which is love, then His work is done and our acceptance lightens not only His load, but ours as well.

At the very end, I had written "ask, accept, what?" Now I knew that the last word wasn't just love as I had written it the first time. Automatically I changed it. Ask. Accept. What? "*Only* love."

Going downstairs to play cards, I was thinking about this experience, still bothered and a little frightened by the whole thing. The words kept ringing in my ears. I sat down at the table and said, I'm going to win. I was absolutely concentrated. And all the other players ceased to exist. I started calling numbers, and the numbers came in as I called them. A pit boss stopped to watch. The money started rolling in to the amazement of everyone. I ran for about ten or fifteen minutes. Finally, the pit boss said, "Pearl, I believe you tonight. We may not have anything left in the whole place when you get through."

As if in a trance, I said, "No, there will be nothing left."

Then a man at the table started kidding around, and I responded. Laughter started all around. We relieved the tension, and at that moment I lost it. It was gone.

The pit boss saw it too. He said, "Pearl, it's gone, isn't it? I was watching you and I noticed when it left."

"Yeh, but I've still got the part that's written down."

The Book

I was in a casino playing cards one day when a weather-beaten face appeared, looking at me with sad large eyes. She spoke, "This isn't kosher and I don't want to hold up your game, but I read your book. It helped me. Thank you so much and God bless you." (She said all of that in one breath.) I responded in love and she left.

Ten, fifteen minutes later a man came around to the side of me. "Miss Bailey, that was my wife you were talking to before. She has been ill for some time. It seemed to us that when she read your book, she was greatly helped. I think she may be actually cured. You see, she has been in a mental hospital, but now she's on her way to clear thinking." The man seemed so full of love, faith, and hope for his wife.

I said, "Tell her, sir, with faith she is cured." I don't know why I said that. I hope something was gained. If so, both the woman and I were blessed.

Audience

Why do they run? What are they seeking? It is love. And with outstretched hands I give it. The young smile and joke. The old look up for hope. Whatever has been given must be shared with all. Not relished, but shared. Love is so frighteningly beautiful.

Why do they cry? Is it for me or them? I choose to think it's for deliverance from despair. I see their souls and I hold them gently in my hands. And because I love them, they weigh nothing. God has set them gently there.

Who said people are a burden? They are a delight. My babies. Yes, they are all my babies, and I shall nurse them with a full breast of love. Take that from me and I shall die.

I feel a great healing power. So when they run up to the stage and we touch, I am healed and so are they. The sickness of hatred and confusion disappear, and we are all free.

I Can't Walk By

Suddenly, as it seems to me, all the races and creeds and nationalities have decided that each person is "somebody." I've done a lot of thinking about this whole situation in America. All I want to know is why did everybody wait so long? Man's recognition of himself should come naturally.

One time a man said to me, half joking, "You have a great inferiority complex." It made me remember that when I was a teenager my sister Eura once called me just the opposite, the snob in the family. I laughed at the time, but it hurt me a little. Actually, I know that I am not a real snob because I could never brush anybody off, if that is what it means to be snobbish. It upsets me to see someone else ignore a person who needs help, because I sense love. I *love* love.

If I see an able person on the street walk right by another who is stumbling or falling in the gutter—actually pass by a fellow man in distress—then that starts me thinking. It's very possible that this is one of the same people who will come to my performances or watch me on TV and admire me. I have to pause there. What I mean is, what happens if I fall out of their favor? Where would I be then? These phonies actually brush off themselves by their action. I do try to avoid people like that. If that's snobbishness, then I guess that I am a snob. As far as I'm concerned, they can wallow in their own juices.

I was at Sardi's one day for lunch, and I decided to saunter back to Sixty-eighth Street where I lived. A blind man—I stopped and dropped in the change. On Fifth Avenue, I passed another blind man, one who is always there with his wonderful dog, standing in one spot. The dog is very old and usually is asleep. When I gave the man some change the dog opened one eye, looked up at me, and went right back to sleep. Wonderful. Yet he's on the job! One look and he knew I couldn't be the enemy.

After a couple of blocks, I saw some teenage kids working the street to sell tickets for something their organization was doing. They were raising money. I stopped and asked. A boy mumbled something about what the tickets were for. Practically nobody was paying any attention to these children. Actually, I figured out that they were from one of the drug clinics, or one of those live-in places where they try to kick their habits. I didn't buy right away, but walked along slowly, thinking about it. Then when I got to the corner where the Schwarz toy store is, I saw an octopus toy in the window, started in, and a fellow stopped me. It was another of those children. "Ticket, lady?"

"What did you say?"

Instead of mumbling, he came out with it more clearly. I started to look for a dollar. Then I said, "No, wait till I come back out. I'm glad I heard you, because the fellow down the street is losing a lot of people. I couldn't understand what he was saying. If you're out here really meaning what you're doing, then open your mouth and say so. Don't be ashamed of it. The shame is over. Right now, you're out here and you're trying for something. Some people will see that and help you."

I went into the store, got the octopus, and came out the side door. After the cool inside the store, the heat started to really get to me. It was one of those hot days in New York. I wanted to get home before the combination of heat and humidity got to me. The doctor had said watch it.

As I crossed the street, I looked back toward the other corner and I could see this fellow up there waiting. I started to turn toward home, and then I started thinking again, "Suppose he's got faith in me, that I'm coming back. I'm wrong to leave." But I kept walking along. When I got to the next corner, there was another one of these kids right in front of me. I looked back. The other one was still in view. The guilt was creeping in. The new boy asked, "Would you buy a ticket?" I was trapped and feeling guilty besides. At this point the boy near the toy store saw me and waved. I turned back to the boy beside me and said, "You know, son, I told your friend over there something, and I don't want to lie to him. He'll see that I'm keeping my promise to come back and buy a ticket."

This one talked pretty well and listened politely while I

rambled on. "I've had some friends who traveled the path with drugs. Really got hung up. I can understand it then because I've seen it up close." (While I was talking to him, I noticed a well-dressed man leaning against a railing. He was watching and listening. I kept talking.) "You're a handsome young man. Your friend over there is young too. I don't know what made you do it in the first place, but it really doesn't matter now. You're on your way out of it. Keep trying to help yourself and others. Keep what I'm saying in mind and go back to your 'house' and tell everybody there it's not worth it." He nodded.

"By any chance did you read my book, *The Raw Pearl*?"

"No."

I reached into my pocketbook and grabbed a ten-dollar bill, the only bill I had on me. I pointed to a bookstore across the street. I said, "Here's ten dollars, go over there and get that book. That's my donation. And you keep the change for the fund-raising, then go to your place and tell your people what the lady said."

A lot of people would assume that the boy would take the money and get some dope, perhaps, but I don't think so.

Now I started to walk away. The man who had been watching us started behind me as I sauntered on. I noticed that he had a large roll of paper like blueprints in his hand. He caught up with me and said, "I saw what you did. I wanted to give something too. But how do you know when to trust them?"

I said, "To tell you the truth, I don't know when yet, mister, but I have a question for you. If all of us refuse to trust them and simply turn them down, then what are their chances for making it back? I have to believe that every man can have a turning point in his life for the good as well as for the bad. For these kids, a turning point for the good means they have to get faith in themselves and in other people who will accept them. They want to live again. If we turn them down, then as far as I'm concerned, we have taken a drug worse than theirs. It's called noncompassion."

The man said, "Well, I suppose you're right, but you never know."

I said, "I don't know who you are, but I trust we're going to walk together in love." We had the nicest conversation, and he walked me all the way to my door. He told me he was a decorator or designer for large office buildings, had a son, and a nice family.

I went down to the Village to see a play called *The Concept*. It's done by ex-addicts who are trying to help themselves and get money to help others. At the end, they go into the audience, kissing and hugging people. They ask, "Do you love us?" Sad, but a much-needed question. I introduced myself to the cast afterward and went into the coffee house next door with some of the actors. It was a pleasant and rewarding evening. I gave everybody a copy of *The Raw Pearl*.

Sometime later, it really knocked me out to see them in the audience at *Hello, Dolly!* They had been allowed to come, along with a sponsor. I introduced them to the audience, and it did me proud to see my fellow actors take their bows, instead of hanging their heads in shame or being shunned by all but each other.

Some days when I arrived backstage at *Dolly* (I always went early), some of those kids would be standing in the corridor. "Remember me? We talk about you often at the 'house.'" One night two fellows and a couple of girls said they had a present for me. It was one of the black soap boxes that they use as simple props in their play. On it were pasted pictures having to do with addiction. For as long as I remained in *Dolly* in New York, I kept that box by the door of my dressing room. Sometimes I sat on it, as they did in the show, to think. And time and again, they came to see me, like hurt babies.

Really, addiction is about the end of humanity in its active form. Addicts will lie or steal or do anything to get that dope, the hard stuff. They say "never again" and then they go back.

An old memory returned from the days when I played the Apollo and went around the corner to eat at Frank's Restaurant. On the way I saw a man.

He was sort of kneeling down on the pavement. His head bent, his hands reaching down as if about to tie his shoe. He was poised in that position, sound asleep. No one else was near as I studied this grotesque statue. He was a young man, and handsome, even with vomit all over his clothes. I wondered to myself, "Dear God, who's going to touch anyone like this?" I tapped him on the shoulder. "Wake up and finish tying your shoes." (I couldn't think of anything else to say.)

He looked up at me, smiled, bent over to obey, and fell asleep again.

Prayer for the Beginning of Each Day

Dear God, please take your fingertips and lift the corners of my mouth at the beginning of each day. Let me smile when the fire of humanity starts to burn hot and would melt your perfect mold. Kindle your fire of love and harden the corners so they cannot drop to scowl.

Deeper grows the ocean . . .

The Children Are Crying . . .

I watch the young generation and their worries worry me. In quietness, my mind turns to them as if by reflex. My thoughts speak to me in troubled words and images. . . . The children are crying and we hear them but we do not understand them—loudly they protest—wrongly and rightly. They are wrong because of the approach they take, the attitude and lack of real truth. They are right because they are seeking these truths and the right approach and the right attitude. And where are we?

We are standing, watching, praying, hating them—

Ignoring them.

Time is passing and they are running out like the tide—deeper and deeper grows the ocean of lost humanity.

They stroll along the quicksand of everyday living, they are sinking and I think they know. Still they are holding hands of love and hope to each other. No strong branches from the rooted oak of truth hang over them. They sink, holding on to each other—forming longer lines every day.

We say the children are to follow us—ha! We are following them—

And not wisely.

They are taking us with them into the quicksand, but we fools are heavier, burdened with time and experience.

Following them, we sink faster.

Their links are real. They know what they are seeking. It's the *where* of it that is throwing them around. We in turn know the what, the why, and the where. Lo! For "what" and "why" we can say. But "where," the one that must not stand alone, slips by us. We know our answers, but we have forgotten to count higher than two—the tape slips back and the count is over.

The direction points one way—down. Afraid—we are afraid to reveal this knowledge, so we increase the pool of quicksand. It grows so large that we cannot straddle it anymore.

Each landing spot in our lives becomes softer and softer.

Like a Breeze, It Brushed Me

I feel the children of today in their loneliness, their search for love, I'd like them to realize that in their loneliness they have company. It happens to almost all young people in their growing up.

I too always wanted love. And now that I have found it I know that it has been there all the time. The directions I sought did not come forth as I wished. And yet, the winds of love could have been blowing my way all the time. Perhaps I had my back turned, or was it my face? Thank God, something in my heart remained open. Somehow, late, a breeze brushed it fully, and the warmth of that breeze created in me a desire to feel the full impact of a typhoon. With my own growth, I became ready to accept love. And you know what?—I haven't been cold for a moment since.

Letter to the Young

Darlings:

Lately I have noticed that you have become my lifeblood. You are my sun and energy. I draw from your warm faces, your searching eyes, your honesty. Strangely, I draw also from your confusion. In it, I find my enlightenment.

I know that your elders and their world confuse you. Maybe that is not all bad. I hope that we will confuse you to the point of curiosity, to the point of searching for more truth and reality than we have found. Yes, more Godliness.

It could be that I am just making excuses. It is, after all, very hard to turn confusion into something good. The most I can hope for is that you will stop sometimes in your searching and ask yourselves—are you truly working toward a world of richer understanding of mankind? If so, then thank you.

Sincerely,
Pearl

Elders: Some Thoughts for the Young

We elders may have reached the point today where we are groping for the aims of you youngsters so hard that we're missing the boat. Sometimes I believe that we don't know how to think about what you are or what you will be.

Truly the majority of the young are seeking absolute truth (take me along, children). I guess in some ways our lives are becoming more sickening to you every day. Many of us want to help you through the quicksand of youth by walking with you, maybe one pace ahead. After all, we know that we have crossed that way before following our own parents or elders. We have stumbled along the path of experience. Do you know that we honestly believe that experience counts for something?

What you feel as quicksand some of us feel as concrete, hardened by the values we learned as we passed. Now don't get us wrong. We know that you will have to harden the path for yourself—your own methods, your own values. Maybe all we can ask is that you have the patience and tolerance to try our ways just once. If our ways are irrelevant, then, as you say, do your own thing.

Each of you is seeking himself. One of the big things you claim to be seeking is you. Turn yourselves on to all life, not just bits and pieces. We believe that in the old-fashioned times of our youth, just every now and then we were you. You may find that in some ways we are still you and you are still us.

Reach

Movies, magazines, and TV are fine. I love them, but in the lives of children they shouldn't replace parents as sources of authority. Parents and children need to sit down these days, maybe more than ever before, to discuss life, not just the horrors. We parents should let our children bring their curiosity to us. These days, a lot of children will read something in the paper or see it in the movies and automatically absorb it and believe it as truth. Even if the report has been factual, youngsters often don't know how to interpret the horrible news that they see. My approach has been to say, "It may be all true and it may be partly true, let's read it together, think about it together, and see what we can gain or lose by it." As we talk, we find that opinions will help both sides. The very active searching is good for us.

One of the things that I have learned in these talks is that the kids are more sophisticated than we are in dealing with some "modern" things. I decided to go to one of the new movies. This one was one of those that goes a bit further than the movies I remember, and it had turned out to be a very attractive movie for the young. I was curious. Would I like the movie? Or would I think that they were doing things simply for shock or to disgust older people? So I went, and I took Tony too. I didn't know exactly what the movie had in it so I had a shock in store. Tony was sixteen and he didn't know anything about the movie either.

We were just sitting there, enjoying the picture, when all of a sudden the sex act started. I tried to see Tony out of the corner of my eye (oh my goodness, what do I do now?). He didn't move at all, but I sort of felt that he was looking at me out of the corner of his eye too. (Mama, you brought me to such a picture!) I noticed that he didn't look too disgusted or too shocked or embarrassed. As a matter of fact, neither of us showed any emotion at all. When the movie was over, we discussed it completely without shame or embarrassment. I told him, "Well, son, I'm sure you realize that if I had known what this was, I wouldn't have brought you." He said, "Mom, I know you wouldn't have, but it turned out all right. Anyway, this summer job of mine—the company does placards for most of the Broadway shows—so I've seen it all anyway."

Where sex is concerned, young people today are very free. Even a movie like I saw, which I'm told was relatively mild, would have made kids aghast in my day. We would have giggled and turned purple around the collar as older people are doing now as they see off-Broadway shows. The children today, however, are very relaxed about these shows. And it is they who find the essential humor in these productions.

I see them going through parks hugging each other, arms around each other. I see them stop in the middle of the street to kiss. These kids seem to have a gentler, more beautiful way of loving than we who are older. The people of my generation claim to be shocked at the sort of thing that is going on on the screen, and yet I think that these same people probably have bigger orgies than any of these children. Give that a lot of thought, folks!

We must stop being hiders and start being seekers— seekers of these people whom we are trying to mold like ourselves. I'd like my own children to be like us in many ways. But the older I get, friends, the more I realize that in some ways I ought to be modeling myself after my children (this will please them greatly). I'd like to get to the point where we could look at each other with frank, loving eyes and accept the fact that God said, "And a little child shall lead them." The young have qualities of gaiety, energy, and strength. We have wisdom, experience, and the stamina to go on. We have the discipline of life. The fun of this thing will be the complete unity between parent and children. A parent wants his children to be good, and you know what is strange? The children want their parents to be good too. We must find ourselves.

Children, don't leave us. We don't know where you are because we haven't looked for a long long time to see where you were going. Perhaps you are now in a fantasyland where we once lived. True, we did not live in it the same way you do, but we lived in that land and it was pretty to us too. Show us the beauty of your world now, but show it to us with kindness. Since you are young, and you still have that great quality of honesty and decency, you cannot really be cruel to us as we possibly have been to you. Give us back ourselves. Lead us. And remember, children, when you reach out for our hands, some of us will accept and some of us will refuse. For some, our grasp in return will be slow because it is so rare to see you reach for us. All this time we have been assuming that we had to reach for you. If any of us refuses, please be patient. Reach harder. Walk up to us and put your arms around us and make us come back to you. If we take the courage to stretch forth our own hands, please accept, don't be unkind. Our love is strong, but we are unsteady. Like you, we have been lost.

Parents, Hear Me

Children are not so frightened by us as we are by them. We can thank our own parents, many of us in this generation, for what they taught us. They may have missed a few things, perhaps they weren't as open with us about some issues as they might have been. But I know that they tried for the good foundations.

Don't hesitate to go woodshedding with your children, if they need it. If you don't do it when they are young, they'll do it to you when they are older. Temporarily they may learn to resent you. Take the brunt of that. They will learn and respect you later. Not only that but they will respect others. It's up to you to help your kids learn to walk among men.

Disciplining Children

When you are kind to the point of violence and cruelty to yourself, and so to the children, then (and it's a hard thing to say) you tread the line of cowardice.

Father and Son

Was it the man or the boy that made me ache inside? The boy was disobedient. The man accepted his disobedience. Okay. The boy is as he is—independent, free, arrogant. The man is sweet, loving, peaceful always and forever. Yet, the man denied the boy the value of receiving what he was looking for—punishment for his disobedience. Not receiving, the boy is unhappy. Unable to give it, the man is unhappy. They are sad for each other, and neither father nor son can make a move to correct this wrong.

Each man has his own way of correcting, granted. But I have watched the boy cry out, "Stop me. Show me that you are the strength." I say to the father, "I am terribly afraid that you have lost some of the boy, some of yourself, and certainly some of me. I forgive, you forget, but the boy remembers."

The Boy and the Man

A boy, all of twenty-five years old, told me that he worked for a man whom he loved and respected. In extolling the man's virtues to me, he said, "I am learning so much from him, but I wish he would learn something from me sometimes." I wondered to myself, what did he want the man to learn? The boy was looking for advice. I knew the boy and I knew the man. So I said, "Dearheart, the better you execute what you have learned from the man, the more he will learn from you, and the more he will teach you. You can teach back the lessons he has taught. Make him see capabilities in you that he did not realize you had. When you have earned the right to talk, he will be willing to listen." Now the terrible part of all of this is that neither the boy nor the man wanted to bow first. That's where the drastic pull always begins. The solution boils down to both people reaching out their hands in a friendly and sincere way to grasp and learn and accept. If you desire someone to grasp your good, and he does, what he returns will be even more than you dreamed he had.

The man should have known that teaching the young can be like driving a horse. If the horse strays slightly to the right of the road, stay with him. If he crosses to the left, steer him gently back. Remember, he's just a bit across the middle line either way. Should he rear his head and revolt, hold the reins firmly. If you let him overturn the cart completely, he can hurt both of you mentally and physically. If he breaks loose and runs away, don't worry, he will return. If not to you, then to someone. Perhaps he will find, as many have, that the end of the road is as far as anyone goes. When he gets there, he will have a decision to make. He might just stand and wait for you to say, "Welcome back, I'll show you the way home." On the other hand, he might feel free and happy away from you.

Boys, like horses, seldom do really bad things if they are given love and discipline.

The man asks, "Did I hold the reins too tightly?"

The boy asks, "Did I resent the bit in my mouth too much?"

It is possible, you know, to hold the reins too tightly, but check this out—only a floundering man holds reins too tightly. I think that when a boy or a horse runs away, he is reacting to the man, not the bit. Horses and boys have a tendency to run away from floundering people. I know the feeling myself, because I too run away from floundering people. Their insecurity frightens me, as it does horses and boys.

Parents

YES, SURE YOU CAN GO. Oh no, she can't. IT'S FASHIONABLE TO GO TO THIS PARTY AND SHE KNOWS IT. Not a daughter of mine. I know she couldn't be home till twelve o'clock and twelve o'clock is too late. DON'T BE A PRUDE. I know that guy who is driving the car tonight. You're crazy to let her go with him. HE'S ACTUALLY A LEVEL-HEADED KID.

SPINACH IS GOOD FOR YOU. It makes her sick.

GET BUSY NOW AND GO CLEAN YOUR TEETH. HOW MANY TIMES DO I HAVE TO TELL YOU? Kids will be kids.

HOW ARE YOU THIS MORNING, HONEY? How do you expect? I guess you want me to say you're right about the kids. Okay, so maybe you're right. THANKS A LOT. I DO WISH THAT YOU COULD REALLY SEE MY METHOD IS BEST. Your ass! LISTEN TO YOUR LANGUAGE. What do you expect? Oh, leave me alone. LET'S SIT DOWN AND REASON IT

OUT. For what? LET'S TRY, JUST TRY. Well . . .
okay.

A BIT OF STRAP IS GOOD. Talking is better. Your way is
nothing but violence. NO, IT'S NOT. YOU'RE TAKEN IN BY
ALL THESE MODERN THEORIES. You're just simply old-
fashioned. WHAT'S THE USE IN THIS CONVERSATION?
Well, the hell with you. I THINK WE COULD WORK IT OUT
. . . If what? IF YOU WOULD JUST TRY A LITTLE
HARDER. Accusing me, huh? OH HELL. See, your pa-
tience is short. I'm the tolerant one around here. WELL,
BULLY FOR YOU. Yeh, but the kids are influenced by you.
THANK HEAVENS FOR THAT. I'd almost say they'd be bet-
ter in a home. YES, BABY, AWAY FROM YOU. Well, I'll
handle the kids from now on. GREAT. And don't you
meddle at all. OKAY, I'LL WEAKEN AND TRY YOUR METHOD,
BUT I KNOW THAT MINE IS RIGHT—A LITTLE STRAP. Some
shit! THERE YOU GO AGAIN. There who goes again?
LOOK, I APOLOGIZE. Okay, I'm sorry too. I DO LOVE YOU.
I love you too. WE LOVE THE KIDS TOO. But of course.
WHY CAN'T THEY LEARN? Who knows? WE TRY SO
HARD. You're right, we do. BUT NO MORE FOOLISHNESS
AROUND HERE. Thank heavens. YOU AND I ARE IMPOR-
TANT. You bettcha!

Where is he? OUT AT A PARTY. And her? ON THE
PHONE, AGAIN. Again? I told him he couldn't go. BUT
THIS WAS SPECIAL, DEAR. I'm expecting an important call.
AFTER ALL, DARLING, SHE DOES HAVE FRIENDS. I thought
we had rules. SO BEND A LITTLE. To whom? TO ME,
THE KIDS. What about me? DON'T BE SELFISH. Who
is being selfish? YOU ARE. Some crap! YOU AND YOUR
FOUL MOUTH. All I say is he shouldn't be allowed to go.

BECAUSE? I'm boss here. ALL RIGHT THEN, YOU LET
HIM GO. You're damn right I will. And I'm going to get a
beer. I'LL GET IT, PASS ME A CIGARETTE. Thanks.
THANKS. This is good. YEH. Well, we try, don't
we? YES WE TRY. Some parents don't. YOU'RE RIGHT.
They'll change. IF YOU USE MY METHOD, THEY WILL.
That's not my theory. SO? Oh, crap! GOOD NIGHT,
I'M GOING TO BED. TOMORROW WE'LL TALK. About whom?
ABOUT THE KIDS. Some crap I will! GOOD NIGHT, LOVE.
Good night.

Love Concealed

Younger, I didn't know him. Perhaps no one did. Perhaps
no one ever will, but somehow I feel I came very close to it. I
missed it by a hair, in the clever way of avoiding the key
issue in his life. He hid it carefully, his vulnerability to her.

He suffered perpetually from the fantastic fear of being
discovered in his love of love. Most of the time he hated
himself for having started that lie in his own life, and as a
result was terribly lonely, shy, and sad.

She motivates his life yet—a praise only for all that's
good for her. Without her, we'd lose a giant, for she is all
he can run to. Once, in fear of losing her, he talked to me.
I was glad, for I felt that if he could see her through, nothing else could hurt him. The rest is all a farce—success,
money, power. Oh, he enjoys the hell out of these things,
make no mistake. But love and warmth from her matter
more. He eats and drinks and breathes his need for her
well-being. I have seen him look at a marquee and feel love
—seen him sit in a dressing room and feel lonely—heard

him knock on a dressing-room door and say thank you for something long done. I wondered why, really, he had come back to talk to me, this proud bully. Then I realized that it was to talk about his love, who then was seven years old.

Pity

I couldn't resist standing there to watch. The emergency squad and ambulance were there, outside the church on Lincoln Road in Florida. The girl lay still. The boy slumped on the back of the emergency truck, "I think she had an overdose." He looked sad for his own generation.

Bearing the girl on the stretcher, the men looked solemn. I supposed that they too had children this age. The girl appeared to be between fourteen and sixteen years old. She was a rag doll—limp, mouth open, teeth broken, and bleeding. She must have fallen, or did someone hit her? Who knows. Bless her heart, whatever the circumstances were, it appeared that she had gone into the church seeking a haven. One could only assume that other doors had been closed. The men pushed the little rag doll into the ambulance and I spoke to them. "Please, if she wakes up, whatever it is or was, tell her it is not worth it. It will never be worth it."

Trip

One child follows another into the drug situation because he materially sees what he spiritually wants or needs—freedom to love and live, express, become real. The catch is that one doesn't need drugs to do this. Walking around without shoes and with hair streaming is wonderful, but it doesn't require a dose of heroin. The only thing one needs is the extreme courage to live fully this given life. That is the simple trip.

Tony and Deedee

Brown-eyed baby, nineteen months, pleasant little boy of four—

Sweet little girl of four months, beauty of two years— and then, suddenly, they are almost grown.—

Why do we have to go to school, or rake yards, or wash dishes, or make up beds?—

What's with this bathing routine, lady? And a boy washing his own socks and underwear, wow!—

A girl of seven learning to set tables and dust?—

You mean we have to tell you where we're going and when and who our friends are? And what's this about getting up when older people come into the room?—

Me home at 11:15? Lady, are you a square?—

You mean we have to leave just because the conversation is not for us, and without a word from you, but only a look? Gosh!—

Ladies first? I thought that was gone.—

Listen to my brother just because he's older? What's with you, lady? What did we do to deserve you?—

Write thank-you notes for gifts received? Drop cards to Aunt So-and-So who is ill? Gee whiz, is this some nut we picked for a mother?—

Did you hear her? She said we were going to Disneyland. I always wanted to see that.—

Hey, these are the kind of neckties I wanted. Maybe she's not so dumb about some things.—

I got an "A" for knowing how to cook. Boy, am I glad she showed me.—

Aunt So-and-So sent me a crazy sweater.—

A cat gave me a job because he said I had good manners. Do you think he's sick?—

Did you see Mom and Dad last night at the music festival? They dug what was going on. Mom looked crazy with those pants and that chain around her waist. And would you believe Dad with sideburns? They sure gassed our friends, and I think our friends gassed them.—

I think they've learned something from us. Could be. I wonder if we learned anything from them. Could be.

Gratefulness

There are lots of gifts in our house at Christmastime. They come from everywhere. Some years ago, it occurred to Louie and me that this might become a problem, especially for the kids. Our family might start taking things for granted. To keep it from happening, we started a special habit in our house, and now observe it every year. Before opening any gifts, each one of us puts a plate beside him. As he opens a gift, each person finds the card and reads it carefully, then puts it on the plate. Soon after Christmas, each person writes a personal note of appreciation for each card on his plate.

This practice takes a lot of time, but I think our kids are beginning to understand that no one really owes us anything at Christmas or at any other time. They feel honestly grateful now to anyone who takes time from his busy life to think of our family at Christmas.

Advice to Tony and Deedee

Running in a circle, someone is in front and someone is behind. Therefore, try to stand in the center. Let the circle revolve around you. Try to be a marvelous pivot. Send out your rays. All your rays will not touch the circumference at the same time. There will be some light and some shadow. But a bit of each is needed by all.

The Young Cabby

Getting into a cab in New York to me is always an experience. It's strictly give and take between me and the driver. Either he tries to talk my head off or he is dreadfully quiet and very fast at the wheel. Sometimes the two of us talk our fannies off. He learns about my business and I accept his problems. He tells me which way is better to go, regardless of which way I want to go. Sometimes he doesn't want to take me anywhere at all. Without exception, these guys seem to be marvelous drivers—great Memorial Day classics. I am awed at the way they skim and skirt in and out of traffic. They make me happy to be alive when I step out on the curb. Every now and then one of these drivers turns out to be a priceless treasure.

His opening line was, "Pearl, are you going into politics?"

"Goodness, no, I hadn't planned on it. But if I would I'd hope to help people and keep whatever promises I made."

He started discussing life. He was going to Queens College part time. I asked, "Oh, didn't they get rid of that?"

"No, we've had our troubles, but on the whole it's still safe. I'm one of the silent majority, Miss Bailey. My father is very conservative."

I asked, "You mean he doesn't agree with your policies, I mean with what the young are doing now?"

"Well no," he said. "Dad came from the Lower East Side and now he lives in a co-op. We're not rich, but it's a big jump from where he was. My father doesn't want anything to disturb his life."

We stopped at a red light. Both of us saw two girls sitting on the sidewalk, no shoes. Another was in the phone booth, wearing blue jeans and with her hair streaming down. Dirty feet. I said, "Son, you wouldn't dress like that, would you?"

"Not really, it's not my thing. I'm against racism, war. Maybe my father just doesn't understand. He's Italian, from the old school, believing everyone in the world that's Italian has to stay strictly within Italian boundaries. I don't enjoy that anymore. I was raised like my father, though, and I admit that a bit of prejudice has crept into me. But, Miss Bailey, you have to live your life like it comes to you. For instance, the other day at work I was taken ill. A colored girl (and he hardly got the word "colored" out before he seemed to stop himself worrying about what my reaction would be) . . . that girl was so kind to me."

I was quiet for a time as we rode along. Then I said, "Are you trying to say, darling, that you could have fallen in love with her?"

"Yes, I am. I could have loved her." His eyes had seen, his heart had seen, and there was love. I said, "Honey, you eat spaghetti and she eats corn bread. If a fuse blows, where does the color go? That's the way it is, son."

He said, "I want to ask you a personal question. When you were with *Dolly* and President Johnson came up on the stage, you were big buddies. Does that mean that you were aligned with him in his policies?"

"Dear boy, I'll tell you, I was aligned with him, and he with me. But then I'm aligned with all humanity. I have admiration and respect for all people." The boy turned around to look at me, seemingly satisfied. When we arrived at the house, he helped me with my bags and shook my hand. Then he smiled and actually kissed me on the cheek. I kissed him too. He had taught me something more about people.

Our Own Thing

Youth, you've often said to me,
"Let us do our thing—
You old ones are not with it."
But I can only say to you
That if you are so with it,
You can and must be who you are,
And take the consequences.

"Our thing" sounds wrong to me, I guess,
For if your self has grown,
It's "my," not "our"; what's you is yours
And evermore you live in part alone.

Once yourself, you cannot help but see
That your own thing and my own thing
Can stand apart and yet be friends—
Secure in singularity.

At Fifty-two

I was walking down Fifth Avenue, strolling rather, with my
hair down blowing in the wind. I was feeling younger than
spring. Three girls, about fifteen years old, stopped me.
They seemed amazed to see me and they made no attempt to
conceal their feelings. I stopped and smiled at them. One
said, "Are you who we think you are?"

Hoping they had the right person in mind, I said, "I think
so, girls." Then I teased them a little—"You didn't know
me, I guess, because I looked so young." (Remember, at
this point, no one had ventured a name.) I went on, "I am
fifty-two and you're worried because I look younger than
you kids do."

They thought about that for about two seconds and then
one of the girls had a beautiful comeback. "You do look
young, but we *are* young." I smiled very broadly at that and
then let go with a good laugh. I said, "You're absolutely
right as far as that goes, but when you say that you are
young, that could be your misfortune." We had a little

game going now. I said, "Now I'm going to have to hit you with a little comeback of my own. I have been young, but have you ever been old?"

In the Park, I Was There

What a lovely Sunday! Just a beautiful day. As I left the health club, I made a decision to take a walk in Central Park which was near my apartment. I had an Indian jacket with long, long fringe, slacks, dark glasses, snazzy hat (one of the mad ones I love). Off I went by myself. I sauntered along.

The children, there they were, mixed in with the older people in Central Park. The older ones seemed to be engrossed in their problems about themselves. The children were engrossed in one another, trying not to have any problems at all. They sat there in groups discussing what? Thinking what? Dreaming of what?

I figured that one way to find out the truth about them was to go among them and ask. Or better still, to go among them and listen. I wanted not to intrude, so I just tried to stand on the side like, possibly, a tree. I didn't want them to be especially aware that I was listening to them. The groups did not stop talking as I grew near, as older folks might have done.

I wanted to be there, but not there. I know that children in particular can sense the attitude of a stranger walking among them. I think that they accepted me because they could tell that I was not simply curious about their lives (that part they call their own). I was there in an attitude of respect, wanting to be a part of their gentle knowledge.

This sensitive quality of a child is something that I've never really lost in my life. If I'm with someone or some group that I can enjoy, I can be completely destroyed if a certain type of person saunters in. Immediately I feel his presence, and I either stop talking or rebel in some way. I definitely resent the entrance. On the other hand, there is another type of person who makes me feel warm and delighted at the very fact that he is near. The difference has to do with what a person brings to a scene. The "draining" person makes me feel afraid. He makes me draw back because I feel that he is coming to take away something and never return or share. When a "good" stranger comes up, I don't consider it an intrusion, even if I never see him again. Because if he takes something good away from my group, I can be pretty sure that he's going to pass it on rather than keeping it selfishly for himself.

Well, I sat on the ground and played with stalks of grass. It was a wonderful day because I watched love in many forms. Dogs of all descriptions ran wild, despite the leash law, and I never saw a single dogfight that day. Some of the youngsters carried little twigs, and others had tiny flowers they had picked. Some were holding hands as they walked along in their wild-looking capes and hats. I saw hair blowing freely in the wind that day. I saw some with shoes and some without shoes, but it seemed that they all had love.

I passed the place where they have concerts in the park. Some lady, bless her heart, was on stage having her own little concert. A few people were sitting on the benches listening to her. Some were resting (closed ears). I have to say that if they were able to sit through this lady's singing, then they really were at peace with themselves and with the world. This woman had the most piercing voice I have heard in some time. But bless her heart, she was delivering to us all, freely and happily. She did encore after encore and no one was applauding. I sat there for a few minutes trying to get the value of what was happening, absorbing every shriek. Even the birds stopped to listen in awe. The smiles, the special looks, and the agony of her free audience were cute to watch.

Then I began to study the lady herself. Her antics and eventually her own admission told me that she was a bit tipsy. She had her own peace going for her. She was doing her own thing, and very happy.

Continuing my journey, I found myself in a huge circle of people. Where all these children came from, I don't know. There must have been five hundred or maybe a thousand of them. They were strumming guitars, playing bongo drums and zithers and harps. I don't know what wasn't happening in that great mass of humanity. They wore all kinds of outfits, and they themselves came in all sizes and shapes. Everyone, if you can believe it, was doing his own thing. I found myself the oldest one there, sauntering among these young people. And they observed me too—the lady in the Indian jacket. It was the same sort of jacket that they like to wear. A few looked at me as if they possibly had seen me before. Others looked at me as if they were only curious about my presence. "Look at the old girl getting with it down here with us." I was smiling inside to be a part of them that day.

I stopped at each little session and watched what was going on. They were lost in themselves. Most everyone I passed smiled and I smiled at everyone I saw. Nobody seemed to ask why we were smiling, we just did it spontaneously, and that was the beauty of it.

Then I went up a slope to a group sitting near the top. Two or three youngsters walked up behind me and asked me whether I was the singer, Pearl Bailey. I gave them an autograph and exchanged a bit of conversation. Then they left and I was sitting there alone enjoying the view of this wonderful mass of humanity.

An interesting sight caught my eye. There was a kite up in a tree, tangled in the limbs. Two fellows were standing underneath the tree discussing Lord-knows-what, and Lord cared not, I am sure. The great thing was that these fellows were at peace with each other. A girl came by and looked up in the tree, long hair dropping down her back. She studied that kite. Heaven knows how long she studied that kite. Maybe she was stoned or completely out of it for one reason or another. After a certain length of time, the two fellows looked at her. She was, after all, a very attractive girl. One thing struck me as rather nice. Neither young man made any fresh comment to her. There was no "How are you? You look good to us." Instead, these young men looked at her and smiled. She smiled and went right back to studying the kite in the tree. Then she decided to get the kite and she started up the tree. After about six inches or so, she fell down. Then she went up about a foot, lost her toehold and fell again. Then she decided she would study the whole situation some more, and she started looking again at the kite.

The young men smiled at her antics. Eventually, she began to walk away, as if to say, "If that's where you want to be, kite, stay there. I have tried." She passed by me. I looked up at her and said, "That was a beautiful thing. I'm writing a book about children and you're going to be in it. I don't know your name, but whenever you read my book, you'll know yourself as the girl with the kite. You took me back quite few years. We used to have kites when I was little. An old newspaper, two sticks, and string. That was it. You have given me back something of myself, something that I had forgotten. I shall include you in my book and in my life." She smiled openly at me and went on her way. I got up, waved good-bye to my little friends up the slope, and went home. I was satisfied, happy. I wish for everyone an experience like I had in the park that Sunday afternoon.

I Have Seen the Master

As I was getting ready to go on stage for a Saturday matinee of *Dolly* at Jones Hall, I saw a little boy standing at Pat the stage manager's desk. Someone said, "Miss Bailey, he's got something for you." I said, "Sweetheart, I've got to go on stage. I can see you after the matinee, but I've got to work first."

After the show, he came back to my dressing room with his little sister. They were the children of the Squires, our promoters. The boy seemed shy, but he presented me with a lovely gift, and one for Dodi, and one for E.B., and another for Roz. Mine was a magnificent red velvet velour case with a silver plaque on top, inscribed, "To the best Dolly." Inside there was a TV set. The gift made me feel warm inside. He said there was a speech he was supposed to make. I said, "I'll tell you what, son. We'll hide this in the dressing room and tomorrow when we're closing the show, you can make your presentation to me on the stage. (Bless his heart, he had his speech so well prepared, I'm sure.) I'll act like I've never seen it before."

When I came out for the finale that closing Sunday, folks went crazy. The cast knew that I was closing more than an engagement. My heart was heavier than I'll ever be able to express. It was a very difficult moment in my life. Yet it was my life I had been playing with. I had gone past pain, gasping for breath, taking medicine upon medicine. I had been to hospitals and doctors and my body cried, "Stop!" I had avoided it as long as I could. I was going to have to rest.

So there we all stood on the stage, filled with emotion. The child came up the side stairs with a huge armful of roses, about three dozen or more. Even as he was walking toward me, he gave me one look and I could see the tears streaming down his face. I led him gently to the center of the stage. By then, he was almost in hysterics. It's enough to see a girl weeping, but to see this boy of twelve so completely shaken up, disturbed me. He held the roses up so that the audience couldn't see his little face and his tears. By now it was a river. His lips trembled.

"What's wrong?" I asked softly. He shook his little head but couldn't speak. I took him back and put him in the line with the cast. Looking into the audience, I saw his mother in the front row, and his sister. His father was at the side of the stage. The remarkable thing is that all of these people were crying too. I looked behind them, into other rows. Even there men and women were crying openly. They weren't even hiding their faces. All over the theater, I heard noses being blown. That's the sound you get in an audience when men are weeping.

Cab turned to the boy and said, "Hi, partner." I said, "Cab, don't bother him." I knew that Cab was trying to do a man-to-man thing to pep him up, but there was no stopping this emotional weeping. I stepped out onto the runway. I said, "And a little child shall lead them. Folks, my lips are moving and I have no words prepared, but the inner voice is saying them through me." I can't remember just what I said, but I remember having my arms outstretched. The child's emotions had filled me too. It was unbelievably powerful, even heavy. I didn't know what to do. So I went around the ramp and pulled him out of the line to me. "Mitchell, why are you crying?" His head was down, his lips still trembling. They got tighter and tighter. The tears pouring. "Don't worry, Mitch, you're a man. It's so nice of you to let us weep with you. Don't think that because you're crying you're a baby. You're not crying anyway, you're weeping. All men can cry, but very few can weep. You're a man." Poor darling. He never made his speech.

In the dressing room a few minutes later, he didn't want to leave. His mother and his sister were still wiping their eyes. His mother said, "Pearl, do you know when you came around the ramp the last time singing 'Hello, Dolly!' that's when he started to cry. He has never done anything like that. He's not one to commit himself so openly."

When he finally left the dressing room, I said to his father, "Do you realize that up on that stage today he was not your son? He was the Master." I knew that I had spent a few moments with the Master, because only He could bring this beautiful ending to something I loved. The boy had made it possible somehow for me to leave and feel no more pain.

After getting some rest and recovering my strength, I went to work the International in Vegas. One night I noticed a child at ringside. Although I move at all times while on that stage, I kept noticing this boy. His eyes were burning into mine, a set smile on his face. He was studying me like a man. At the very end of the show, I leaned over to shake his little hand, and this boy calmly took a giant step, never looking back at the people behind him. And he was on the stage. I stopped dead. People were laughing and applauding. Suddenly I stretched my arms out wide. He stretched his, and simultaneously we clasped one another. I didn't stoop over, but somehow this little boy reached up and kissed me on the cheek. I have wondered since then, how did he get that tall?

Now, to get to my dressing room, one must go down through a labyrinth. You absolutely can't get there unless you know very well where it is. When I got down there, I was quite shaken by the power of that boy on stage. There was something strange about the whole thing. Jeannie sensed it. She asked, "What's the matter?" I said, "I saw the Master."

"What—where?"

"Upstairs, Jeannie." I told her about the child. Then there was a knock on the door. Jeannie went to answer it and when she came back, tears were starting from her eyes. "What's the matter?" I said.

"He's there."

"Who's there?"

"The Master." I walked to the door, and there he stood, alone. He stepped inside the room and a couple of minutes later his father caught up with him. He had made the trip by himself. I sat in a chair opposite the father. The boy stood at his right. There was a strange air in the room. I asked the boy to get me a tonic water from the icebox. I wanted to talk to the father. When the boy stepped away, I said, "You know what happened on stage, don't you?"

"Yes," he answered very quietly. "Something strange happened. I felt it."

"Do you realize, sir," I asked, "that tonight that boy is not your son. That's a very old man at the icebox."

He said, "All I know is something happened between you and him."

"Sir, you can't touch it, can you?"

"No, I can't," he answered. "Maybe his mother didn't see

it, but I did. When you left the stage, my son got up from our table and no one moved. There was quiet all over the room, absolutely no one moved. The impact was overwhelming for everyone." We were almost whispering by now. I said, "I'll tell you. I would say he is older tonight than all the people in that room put together. An old man, not a boy."

Now the boy brought the soda over, not speaking. He stood for a moment and then said, "Do you have a rest room?" I got the distinct feeling that he did not want me to go too far. He didn't want to hear what I was going to say. I pointed to the rest room in the back. He stayed back there a long time. I continued my talk with the father.

"He's around twelve hundred years old," I said. "Are you Hebrew?"

"Yes, I am."

"What is the Hebrew year?"

"I don't know, but my wife's a teacher. She's still upstairs. I think she'll know." He called, but she didn't know. This took a bit of time. As soon as it was over, the child came back. I said, "Oh, son, we were just talking about you."

"What did you say?"

"I told your father you were around twelve hundred years old. But now I say fifty-six or fifty-seven hundred and some-odd years. Your father doesn't know the Hebrew year . . ." He interrupted me, "It's fifty-seven hundred (and he named the odd years)." I asked him, "How do you know?"

"They teach it in the Hebrew school, but I know how old I am."

I walked into another part of the dressing room where the bed was. The boy sat on the bed and I sat on the floor. His father stood at the door. Now I wanted to talk with this person and hear more. We spoke briefly and then the father interrupted. He said, "My wife's on her way down here. She has never been in a star's dressing room." I had a flashback to the night before when I had said to Jean, "It burns me up when people call me a star. I don't like that because stars are in the sky. Human beings are on the earth." I turned to the father and said, "Sir, she's not going to make it tonight because I'm not a star." I turned to the boy and said, "What do you say to that, son?"

He said, "Stars are in the sky." It really shook me up.

When the mother arrived she was all excited. I said, "Lady, do you know that you have an old man here? He's not your son tonight." It was as if she hadn't heard me. She said, "Oh, look at this dressing room." She began to talk about my decor and the enjoyment of the theater and all sorts of things. In the midst of this I saw a fantastic thing happen. The old man became a boy again. He said, "Can I have your autograph?—I'd like to have a soda.—Is that your record player?" I saw it happen before my eyes. He realized that his father knew and his mother didn't.

The river has
stopped building . . .

Mama's Hats

I was walking down Madison Avenue when a man stopped me. "Miss, are you Pearl Bailey?"

"Yes."

"I knew your mother. Lived on her third floor. She treated me like a son. I remember her as a warm and wonderful woman."

He went on and on. That was Mama, all right.

I am lonely for Mama, but it isn't that great loneliness that I feared it might be. It is not the loneliness of tears. She is, after all, so very much alive in her impact on my life— and my memories of her.

Sometimes when I have a particularly exciting experience, I find myself saying, "Mama should see this." (I know how she would take things.) All my life I never really thought of her as Mother in the sense that some people think of a parent. I thought of her more as a great woman, a fine actress without knowing it. Every move was a picture. On stage, I sometimes find that I am Mama. It was true in the picture, *The Landlord*, when I graciously and grandly put ham hocks in the lady's purse—"Do eat honey"—that's exactly what Mama would have said.

Near the end of Mama's life, I went to Philadelphia from New York to see her every day. I was working in *Dolly* and so had to go back and forth. When I arrived at her house, the nurses would bring her downstairs. Mama always wanted to sit in the kitchen, and it's my favorite room in the house too.

Sometimes her thoughts would stray. She would be talking away about something serious and the next minute her humor would flow.

We children would always use the occasion to bestow great love on Mama. Now I was never the "kisser" in the family. Willy and Eura, yes. Virgie was about like me. But suddenly toward the end, sitting in the kitchen, all of us became "love bugs." All the while we were growing up, Mama had never been a woman to pull and hug her children, always asking, "Do you love Mama?" Instead, she just sat back and waited when she knew her work was done. I guess she always wanted to know that the affection came out naturally. Yet, in those last weeks when I'd come to see her, she'd be sitting at the table waiting for her loving. A beautiful picture of a woman. When one of us would lean over and kiss her on the face, she would just beam, and those dimples always came into view.

I found out that Mama just loved it when I put my hats on her. So every time I went in, I'd take my hat off and put it on her head. Do you know, she never removed one of them? Eventually a nurse would have to take it off after we left. I remember saying to her several times, "Now you really think you look like something in that hat, don't you?" Right away, the smile and dimples. I'd say, "You're gorgeous, Mama." And I always had a feeling that part of her smile was at me, because I had become a big kisser all of a sudden.

The first time she had to go into the hospital, she wore one of my hats, going and coming. The second trip required an ambulance because she was an emergency case. Still, in and out of the ambulance, in the wheelchair, up and down the steps, there she was with one of those hats. Finally, when the ambulance pulled up to the door for the last time, I was wearing Mama's favorite hat of all, a blue one. Mama sat at the head of the stairs in her wheelchair, waiting to be carried down. As she went by me at the front door, I popped the blue hat on her head. Then, as she waited to go down the front steps, I lifted the brim of the hat and looked underneath into that tiny face. She kept that hat on, even lying down in the ambulance.

A week and a half later, I went over to the hospital for one of my regular visits, and I had on a new hat—a big Panama with an orange band around it. Mama was sitting up in the bed, with her head sort of bowed. Leona, her nurse, said, "She's in a good mood today." I approached Mama and put the big Panama on her head. She didn't move or make a sound.

"Mama, do you like that one?" No answer.

I asked her again, but still got no answer. I couldn't even see her face, just that hat with the brim down over her eyes. I said to the nurse, "I thought you said she was talking and laughing." Frankly, I was beginning to get a little alarmed. Leona said, "She was."

I thought, Dear God, has she sat here and died? Then I reached out and lifted the brim of the hat. Mama looked up and gave me a big smile, then threw back her head and laughed so hard it surprised me. Throwing her head back to laugh, she crushed the hat. Jesting, I said, "Mama, you're crushing my beautiful hat." By this time, the hat was falling off, so I picked it up and put it back on myself. I also was wearing an orange and black necktie and an Aries pendant.

Mama stared at the hat, and then started to pull on my necktie, then grabbed the pendant. Her eyes finally settled, riveted on the Aries. I really had to hold on to the other end of the necktie to keep it on. Still she was staring.

It was past time for the regular nurse to show up. I walked to the door two or three times, not wanting to leave Mama alone. (Mama, how did we know that was it?) Her eyes studied my hat again, but were they moving?

"Mama, I'll be back." I stepped into the hall, glanced back into the room, then stepped out and found a nurse. "Will you watch her until the regular nurse comes?" She said she would.

I had to leave. As I went through the door of the hospital, I passed her nurse coming in. They would call me if there was any change. I arranged the big Panama and headed for New York.

I remember that I knew the curtain was coming down. The next thing I knew I was in Doctors Hospital. What happened in between has been filled in by my friends. I fainted right on the stage, and was laid out in the white closing dress while they waited for doctors. Someone must have called Joannie Hodges, who left Brooklyn with a doctor at once. Then there was an ambulance and I wound up in Doctors Hospital. At the hospital, half awake, I told Doctor Hitzig, "Mama is dying." (We were waiting for the end sometime, but had no time clock on her life.) Doctors were around my bed, and then there was sleep.

When I woke up, I was climbing over the foot of my bed. Why, I have no idea. A nurse came in and said firmly, "Get back, Pearl." Childlike, I obeyed. Later, Doctor Hitzig came back. "How are you, Pearl?"

"Fine. My back hurts, Doc, right here." Why didn't he

seem to be listening to me? Why was he watching me so strangely?

"Pearl," he spoke, "did you say your mother was dying?"

"Yes, Doc."

"When did you say she was dying?"

"I don't know, Doc, how do I know?"

"Pearl, she's dead." I bounded out of the bed. He told me not to get excited. I said, "I'm not, Doc, I'm just putting my clothes on to go to Philly. Call home, bring me some clothes."

I got downstairs and found Joannie waiting in the hospital lobby. She had been there all night. What a woman! Then I was off to Philly, straight to the hospital.

Requiem

The lasting significance of those who have passed is that they have lived. They live on in some form as an example that God produces. They sleep as a sign that God also rests one. If I should find a body on the street, regardless of the circumstances of the death, I could only look and say, "He lived." Some people would ask, "Where has he gone?" The only answer I need is, "Beyond us." I have lost four loved ones in the last two years, but I cry neither for the ugliness of it, nor for the beauty of it. I think the thing that bothers people in thinking about death is that for once they know there is nothing they can do about something. Man can only recognize that in death there is an end to man's selfishness and hurt—the weaknesses that man must live with.

As Papa passed in 1966, his eye was open looking at me. I didn't even know when he died. In his eye I saw life and death and understanding. I saw something that said to me, "I have set my eye on you and I look deep into past, present, and future." I saw all of myself in that eye.

Mama's death spoke to me too. I am still grasping the meaning of that experience for me. When they told me that Mama was dead, I got up from the hospital bed and headed for Philadelphia. Joannie Hodges was with me. I went directly to the hospital, thinking perhaps the family would be there or I would see Mama before they moved her from the room. I found that they had removed her before I arrived.

I remember asking the nurses, "May I go into that room and sit for a while?" They nodded. I had on that same Panama hat that Mama liked so much, the one she had enjoyed during my last visit with her. Joannie stayed outside and I went in alone. I sat down in the chair at the foot of the bed. I looked at the bed all made up and clean and thought, "Mama was lying there with my hat on. Mama's not there anymore." I just looked around. Air hammers were going outside the window. When they had brought Mama in, this was the only room they could find in the emergency. Later, I recalled, they wanted to remove Mama upstairs to a quiet room with a private bath. I had refused, saying, "No, I don't think the family would want her moved around anymore. I don't think she hears the noise anyhow." I knew that even if she heard it, it wouldn't bother her. Mama never was a complainer. She stayed in that room. Now I sat there in silence. Soon Joannie crept in beside me and we both sat quietly for a time. Then we both knew that there was nothing else to do. It was over.

Mama had never wanted to go to a doctor, let alone to stay in a hospital. When she got so sick and they put her in, they had a pretty hard time with Mama. Come to think of it, Papa was the same way. They couldn't get Mama to take her medicine. There were three nurses, Dorothy, Ruthie, and that darling Leona (the one who was with her when she died). Mama conned those nurses all over the place. In her babbling, she said things to those girls that weren't in the book. She kept them in stitches most of the time. Here was a woman who was going on to better things, but was still one of the greatest actresses of all times.

One of the nurses would give her a pill, then ask her a few minutes later whether she took it. She could always make them believe that she had taken a pill that she was still hiding someplace. Sometimes Mama would take off her ring and put it in her mouth. Now that really gave the nurses some concern. First of all, they didn't want her to swallow it. Mama had somehow gotten the idea that the nurses were after her ring for good. She remained quite good-natured about it, but the nurses simply couldn't get the ring out of her mouth. I helped them get it back because I had given her the ring in the first place. We gave it to Eura to keep.

Mama spent a good many of her last hours on this earth thinking about Governor Nelson Rockefeller. I think she seized on that because on the wall by her hospital bed she had a picture that showed me and the Governor. I had been chosen the Woman of the Year for the U.S.O. For the presentation, Jeannette Rockefeller was Chairman, and the Governor came on the stage with me to dance and sing on award night. I had given the pictures to Mama while she was still at home. When she had to go to the hospital, she insisted that the pictures go with her.

Now the funny thing about all this is that my Mama was a staunch Democrat. All of a sudden, she could think of no one but Rockefeller. She told the doctors and everybody in sight about how important she was because she knew

Rockefeller. She did not know Rockefeller. Anyway, she had it fixed in her mind that Rockefeller was coming to her house for dinner, and she had to cook for him. My mother was an immaculate housekeeper, and she was really worried about getting home in time to put everything straight. When we would visit her she would say, "Get home and get busy. All four of you children know how I am about being clean. I don't want that man in my house if things aren't just so." We tried to tell her that everything was straight. I remember once she came back again, "You're standing here looking into my face, Pearlie, Willie, Virgie, Eura, telling me everything is straight when you should be downstairs cleaning the house for Governor Rockefeller."

I turned the whole thing around on her just once. She had refused to take a pill. The doctors and nurses had a try at it. And finally in desperation I said to her, "Mama, please take the pill because Governor Rockefeller is coming to dinner. We're going to fix something for him. If you don't take this pill, he probably won't show up for dinner. As a matter of fact, right now he's out there in the hall, but I know that he won't come in here unless you take this pill." I hate to tell you what she answered, Governor, but she said, "The devil with Rockefeller. If he wants dinner, he can come in here and cook it himself!" One Sunday when I went over to the hospital, she was thinking about President Nixon. That was a switch. She said, "You know, Pearlie, that Nixon is going to be all right." And I looked at this staunch Democrat and said, "Mama, you think so?" She said, "I think he's going to be all right, and he's going to get on the ball." I said, "Mama, you mean you think he's getting ready to get in business?" She said, "Oh yes, he is." (Her eyes went up to the ceiling.) Suddenly she dimpled up, smiled, and said,

"Yes, Nixon's going to all right, but I'll tell you one thing. He'd better hurry up and do it if he's going to do it at all."

Aside from Rockefeller and Nixon, the main thing that occupied Mama's mind in the hospital was her obsession for getting back home to take care of the house. My mother was the kind who would unmake beds if no one had slept in them so that she could make them over again. That's how neat she was. It may have been unfair of us children, but we once sat down in the lobby and discussed it. "Mama is very very sick. Is it possible that she is putting the house before God? Is she that obsessed?" We were just worried, that's all. After a while, Mama started performing so that we had no choice but to get her out and take her home. It was a decision made by the family together. I did want Mama home. I had never known her to be out of the house. Yet I knew that we did not have the facilities at home to treat her condition. Anyway, they took her home and did the best they could.

I went back to *Hello, Dolly!* because I had to. Then Mama developed a 104° fever. They called and said they were bathing her down. Louie and I caught the train for Philadelphia and got in about two in the morning. When we got to the house, there was this little frail creature. We debated where to put Mama so that she would be most comfortable and we could care for her more easily. At my suggestion, we moved the dining-room furniture out and put her in there, hospital bed and all. We knew that Mama wouldn't care for the idea because she didn't believe it was proper to see a bed when you opened the front door. We solved that problem by putting up a screen.

They bathed Mama trying to hold that temperature down. It went back up again and again. The poor little thing was shivering and her eyes had lost their meaning. After being in the dining room for just so long, some of us would step into the kitchen to have a cup of coffee and sit there staring into space before walking back to the bed. At times she showed no recognition when we rubbed her forehead and her fingers. She was getting worse. About six in the morning the nurse called the doctor and we thought it was the end. He showed up about forty minutes later (it seemed more like forty years). "Take this woman immediately to intensive care." They called police emergency and we knew there was not much hope. It really got me to see two policemen arrive to get Mama, instead of a regular ambulance coming for her. The policemen had a basket and a blanket. All I could imagine was that a basket is to put bodies in when people have passed. Our darling mother, carefully they put her in the basket. I leaned against the kitchen door. Lou was standing there. I'll never forget Mama's eyes as long as I live. She had small eyes anyway, and now they made her look like a little lost bird. Silent, she seemed to ask me, "What are they doing to me, Pearlie? Somebody is doing something to me, but what? Are they taking me away?"

I choked, "Oh God." Those eyes had told me all I wanted to know. I had seen the same look in my Papa's eyes. I knew it was Mama's last trip from Twenty-third Street.

We were all completely drained from the tension. I was especially troubled because I had had a misunderstanding with one of my sisters, and she had left the house. When I had seen her marching out of the house at that crucial time, I had gone to the door to try to call her back. She had kept walking, and that was preying on my mind.

Everyone dashed out behind the ambulance, but I remained to call my sister. "They've taken Mama away. She's much worse." I was sitting in the hospital waiting when my sister arrived. I put my hand on her shoulder and said, "Don't worry, everything is going to be all right." She just stared at me with that look. I asked, "Are you still angry?" I was thinking, "Is it me? Is it an accusation she is making?" Then my sister screamed a loud, piercing, heart-rending scream. Instinctively, I clasped my hand immediately over her mouth. We were, after all, on an intensive-care floor. I just wanted to shut off that sound, and then release her. Before I could do anything, bedlam broke loose. She slumped to the floor. Someone yelled, "Move your hand so she can breathe." My hand was moved. What were they talking about? Nurses and doctors came from everyplace. She was out cold. I knew that she had had a little trouble with her heart, and I was terrified. They wheeled her into an emergency room. I stood there thinking, "Can it be that they are both going?" As it turned out, she revived quickly. She had only fainted, and there was no complication with her heart.

Sitting by that clean bed in the hospital, I went over all of this in my mind. Then there was nothing to do but leave. I had the funeral home to think about. We made preliminary arrangements, and then I had to get back to New York for a day. When I came back for the viewing, I had to pass Reynolds Funeral Home where Mama was resting. With me, I had the children, Aunt Lucille, Dodi, and PeeWee. We stopped and I asked the others to wait. "Let me look alone." I wanted to feel all the hurt and see if I could take it. I really didn't know what I would feel when I saw Mama lying there. This time she was not in her bed at home, and I knew that for the first time she wasn't going home. Slowly, Pearl.

"She's not ready yet," the man said. "We've been waiting for you to pick the things."

"Pick what?"

"We have dresses in stock, and everything you'll need." I didn't know what "stock dresses" meant in this case. He said they had different sizes.

"Oh, I thought everyone brought their own dresses. Anyway, mister, we've got to dress Mama ourselves." I selected a beautiful bronze casket and then went on to the house. We sat around the kitchen table. Eura, Willie, Virgie, and Mr. Walter, who was sick himself at the time. Nobody really knew what to say or do. I didn't want to pull out that picture of the casket, not yet. Finally, I said, "What color dress would you like Mama to wear?" Someone said yellow. Mr. Walter was cute about this, he chose red and some people agreed with him. Virgie wanted blue. And blue it was.

The telephone rang, and it was Dodi. I'll never forget this girl as long as I live. She had just gone home to California after a long stay in New York with me. When she arrived in California, she got the news. Now, all she had to say was that she was on her way to Philadelphia. No one even had to ask her. That's Dodi. Mama always adored Dodi, and vice versa. "Never mistreat Dodi," Mama said, "because she's my girl—we're both Jewish." We had lots of good laughs with Mama about that one. I told Dodi that we needed a beautiful blue dress, so she went to New York first and picked it out. It was exquisite. With that and her silver slippers, Mama was materially ready. Spiritually, there was peace on her face.

We went back to the funeral home over and over. I realized that Mama didn't have lipstick on. I gave her a kiss, leaving just a slight trace of my own lipstick on her lips. Beautiful. My head was spinning with fragmentary thoughts, "I'm not afraid, Mama, I'm not afraid anymore of life. Death is beautiful. The peace that passes all understanding. Your face tells me so. You have not left us. You are here, but sometimes I'd like to talk to you materially. You hear, don't you, Mama? Do you?"

The people started coming. First there was the family. Mama was so gorgeous that she outshone everyone. Her personality seemed strong even in death. Standing by the casket, I acted as the hostess, smiling and comforting each person who came (I was lying, Mama, at that moment). I was so hurt, and someday I know it's all coming out. I spoke with the people, and I gazed at all the beautiful flowers from friends and strangers alike. When everyone else had gone, I stayed with Mama because I wanted to keep company with her. We had things to say. Then too I knew that Mama would have had a fit if she had thought someone wouldn't be there to greet a possible stranger who might drop in. Someone had to be there just in case to say, "Thanks for coming." That's the way Mama would have done it. I'm glad I stayed because, in fact, more people did come. All her nurses from the hospital. After a moment, one of them turned to me and said, "You're going home to get some rest." It took me a long time to convince them that I was all right—that they should just let me stay with Mama. The nurses had grown very fond of her, even to the point of calling her "Mama." Leona started feeling faint, and had to get smelling salts from her purse. In good humor, I said to her, "You're trying to send me home, but if you don't stop fainting, I'm going to take your smelling salts away and your nurse's cap too." Nurses are supposed to keep their composure at all times, seeing life and death so often, but Mama had increased their values too.

I remember wondering why I was all so calm. "Am I in a play? Is this real?" I asked myself. I know that I wasn't as composed as I must have seemed. Doc Strickland had been sneaking looks at me earlier in the day as if to ask, "When does she drop?" Looking back, I would say it's probably the only way I could get through with it at all, the only way.

When I finally returned to the house, there was a man sitting at the dining-room table. He was Papa's identical twin, Uncle Frank. I had only seen him once before. He said, "I'd like to see the baby girl, Pearlie."

I said, "I'm Pearlie, and I've been waiting a long time to see you, Uncle Frank." He was Papa's last living brother. When I was about thirteen or fourteen years old, Uncle Frank showed up for the first time, never having seen any of my father's people. I saw him as a very special, romantic, benevolent kind of man who had come from nowhere. He had come in planning to move to Philadelphia. "Well, well, here's my brother's child." Boy, did he look prosperous to me then. He decided to give me a present.

Well, he moved to a house near the twenty-two hundred block in South Philadelphia, and we lived at 1900 North. You had to pass Market Street to even start counting for South Philadelphia. "Send her down Saturday, and I'm going to buy her a pair of shoes." Terrific, a rich uncle has shown up and I'm the favorite. After he left, Mama said, "Frank does not keep his word, so don't be too disappointed if you don't get those shoes." When Saturday came, I got on the streetcar anyway. Tokens were two for fifteen cents. One of my sisters was going with me, so Mama gave us just two tokens. She said Frank can give you the tokens to come home. We were off on the number 33 streetcar, pleased as Punch. When I finally arrived at his door, with my heart beating fast, I knocked but got no answer. I had to walk all the way back home to North Philadelphia. The shoes I had on were completely worn out.

Now Uncle Frank wanted to know, forty years later,

which one was "baby Pearlie." "Okay," I said, "Where are my shoes?" Nine months later, Uncle Frank dropped dead.

Virgie and I packed up Mama's clothes. I found myself hugging some of them to my face warmly. Willie moved the furniture. I don't think Eura could have taken any of this. The house is sold now, and it's all over. After I'd packed Mama's belongings, I never re-entered the house. I wonder whether I would have been afraid. Would I? I really think that I might have broken up. I needed some time to work things out.

Just the other night, I was lying in bed, and goodness gracious, a strange feeling came over me. "It's been a year since I've seen Mama. How I want to see her now. Oh, well, I'll drop by home the next time we're in the East."

She left a powerful legacy to me. I always wanted to be near her as much as I could. Once when I was working and living in Greenwich Village, I called and said, "Mama, I'm coming over." I had a day off and this is how I wanted to spend it.

"Oh, Pearlie, don't come today because Mama's hanging her curtains." Sometimes that would make me boil inside. I couldn't stand the thought of being rejected by Mama even for a day, even if she was hanging her curtains. Couldn't she hang her curtains with her own child in the house? I guess we all remain children in some ways forever where our Mamas are concerned. The funny thing is that today, I do the same thing to other people sometimes. "Dearheart, not today, I'm busy." There were times when Mama was busy doing her own thing.

I understand now that I have a house and responsibilities of my own. When I tell anyone I'm busy, it's because I'm cleaning my house or doing something simple that is never-theless important to me. Mama had really made friends with her house. She loved the neatness and the beauty of it. When her work was done, she would sit in the living room, cross her legs, and enjoy. I remember going in and saying, "Mama, how are you?" She said, "I'm fine. Let Mama show you the cellar, what I've done. There's a table down there now and a comfortable chair. Oh, Pearlie, it's spotless." Sometimes in our selfishness we children would tell her it wasn't important how the cellar looked. Children do this to their parents sometimes.

Today, I have the understanding. I know everything she was doing in that cellar. I know what she meant when she said, as she often did, "I'm keeping a home for you all so you'll always have a place to live. You never know what you'll come to in life."

That's the reason even the cellar mattered to Mama.

Settling Mama's Estate

We sat in the lawyer's office in Philly, getting our settlement that Mama left us. It was especially nice there because there were no undercurrents between us children. All of us were feeling the great loss of Mama. It hadn't been so when the will was read originally. Each of us was lost in his own hurt, his private thinking. That made a strain for some reason, I don't know exactly why.

But September 1, 1970, was good. We were laughing. As a matter of fact, the lawyer himself was in stitches. His secretary said that she had never laughed so hard in her life. I think that both of them were enjoying our unity. We were understanding each other a bit more, all grown up now.

For being the executrix of the will, the lawyer gave me

something more. "Pearl, here's an extra check which comes to you by law."

"A check?" Immediately it hit the pit of my stomach. I didn't want anything from Mama. There was a long silence. No response. Thank God, nobody seemed angry that I was getting something more. The smiles didn't disappear. All Mama's children chorused together, "We understand. The love was there. Mama would have liked that." Right then I divided my extra part by four. I had done no more than was right, so I deserved no more a part of my mother's bowels than my brothers or sisters.

I thought how wonderful it was that this generous Mama of ours was still providing for us in a way. Surely if we had had no food or money, this little gift she left for us would have kept us going for quite a while. Her picture hangs in my kitchen in New York and in my office in California. We talk often, Mama and I. And sometimes we just smile at each other. Mama, it's done now, it's all done. Peace.

Tears Not There

Sylvia, a dear friend, caught my show six times at King's Castle. Six times she wept when I did a song called, "Mama, A Rainbow." As she wept openly, I wept singing and wept inside.

As I did "When the World Was Young," I always remembered Mickey, a dear lady now gone. That memory always brought a smile. Like schoolgirls, we were laughing in July of 1969 in a booth at the International Hotel. Then no more. Now the words to that song bring happy memories and take away sadness. Papa, Mama, Mickey, and Mr.

Walter all departed in eleven months of 1969 and 1970. In a strange way, it bothers me to realize that I have not shed tears. Why aren't I weeping yet?

As I sit here and look at the glorification of God in the mountains, lakes, and trees, I ask, "Lord, why don't I feel sad? Is it that I don't love these people, and miss them? Each one was wrapped around my bowels."

I haven't talked to Mr. Walter's family. And I haven't been back to Mama's house since it was sold. I must go have a cup of coffee with the lady who bought it and sit in Mama's kitchen again. Miss them? Yes, Lord, I miss them. Care? I care, and yet I have no tears. The four are gone, but they are at peace.

Judy

Usually when I close a job in Vegas, I pack up and leave town right away. As often as not, I've got to be someplace pretty quick. One time, however, I just pushed everything else out of the way and stayed where I was. The reason was that Judy Garland was due to open in Vegas after more than a year away. Judy had had lots of trouble, and the rumors were flying. Anyway, rumors or no rumors, here was my first chance to see Judy perform in vaudeville. The chance was too good to miss.

For her opening, I was there at a ringside table. It seemed to me that every agent, manager, friend, and enemy in show business had come to see her. They came from both coasts and points in between, and it looked like Who's Who in show business. After her first number, there was decent applause, but there was a strange quiet in there too. After her second number, she had gained some ground. The applause was better, more natural. The tension was letting down. Then she came out with "How About Me?" by Irving Berlin. "It's over, all over, and soon somebody else will tell the world about you—but how about me?"

Hearing the way she sang that song made my heart drip tears. From where I sat, I could see that sweat was pouring off her little face. And it wasn't that hot in there. She was confident, and at the same time afraid. I knew that she couldn't be afraid of her talent, but was probably more afraid of her life.

As she received her applause, which was thunder, she was standing at the railing above my table. I don't know what compelled me, but I reached over and took Louie's handkerchief from his coat pocket and passed it up to Judy. She leaned over and I said, "You've spent thirty years up there, and I know they'll give you at least a minute to wipe your face." Actually almost everybody heard me say that, because when the audience saw us touch, they fell silent, and my voice carried the room. Lord knows, I didn't intend that. Laughter came. Wonderful laughter, warm and friendly. And the room became loose. Judy took that place by the corners and shook it, caressed it, and turned it upside down as she went through her program. Then she came toward the end, her "Tramp" number with her funny costume and her red polka-dot bandanna. When she finished the show, she came forward to take her bows. Then, with the audience still out of their minds, she turned. And as she was leaving, paused to reach and put something in my hand— her red bandanna hankie. And she was gone.

God had given us a reprise to see Judy again. She died in London and her body was brought back to New York to lie in state. That morning around seven or eight (I was working on the film, *The Landlord*, and therefore had to be up early) I went to deliver a letter to the side door for Liza, her daughter. I felt that Liza would be needing comfort. People had been in line all night. There were the barricades and photographers. When I delivered the letter, I found myself being ushered inside before I knew what was going on. I hadn't really intended to go in near the casket. The guards stopped the line, and I approached. Judy was tinier than ever, like a doll baby. A tiny doll.

Mickey

Her niece opened the door, and after greeting me, said, "We expected her to be gone last night." Was it really that bad? Was my friend who looked so beautiful in July really dying in December?

Silently, I went into her room. Her frail back was turned, and her knees were raised in a sitting position. "Mickey? Mickey?" I spoke softly. Then she turned to face me. I could hardly move. Her small, lovely face was thin and frightened. Her eyes, always so large and alive, were absolutely alone in her face.

"Pearl," she said, "I'm dying."

"Mickey, God is selling you something. Are you buying it?"

"I'm buying it, Pearl."

"Then Mick, realize that he has no bargains, it's all first class."

My arms were filled with hers and Fred's Christmas presents. It was Christmas Eve morning. "Mick, do you want me to open your presents?" (Poor nut, me, I didn't know what else to say.) "No, Pearl." I gently placed them all around her.

Suddenly, she had pain, or shall it be said, more pain. Her niece brought a pill.

For a while I went into the kitchen to have coffee and talk with her niece. She told me Mickey had asked for her family, some from St. Louis and some from Los Angeles. They were on the way. Again, she told me that they had expected her to die the night before. I put my hands to my mouth in a gesture that said, "Be quiet, or she'll hear us."

"Oh, she can't hear." I told her, "Yes she can, too."

Going back to Mickey wasn't easy—that agonized, yet knowing face. She knew very well what was happening. "Pearl, I'd like to turn over and get up higher on the pillow."

"Okay, Mick."

"But you can't raise me. Even Fred can't raise me."

"But I can, Mick." Putting both knees on the bed, I put my hands underneath that tiny body—her stomach bloated, her limbs tiny—and heaved away. One, two, and up she went, with her head on the pillow. "Better, Mick?"

"Oh, yes—wrong medicine, Pearl, wrong medicine. I asked for my family last night, Pearl, to say good-bye. I'm dying."

"Mick, do you want me to wash you?"

"No, Pearl."

"Do you want to rest, Mick?"

"Yes." I remembered for her our visit to the Savoy Plaza for dinner. She smiled about that. We had laughed there. Then, "Pearl, will you see that I am clean?"

"Yes, Mickey. Now rest. I'll be back tonight."

I was in rehearsals through the day. When they were over, Lord, the fatigue took me over. Louie, the children,

Nick, Jean, and I stood in the lobby. I was debating with myself whether to go to Mick or to go rest myself, and then go see her the next morning. I went upstairs with Louie. He was insisting that I get some rest. With my hat still on my head, I flopped in a chair. Suddenly I decided no. "I must go, Lou." And off I went.

I got into a cab. At holiday time, Vegas is loaded with traffic, people rushing to everywhere—to the tables and to the shows. Traffic stopped as an ambulance screamed by us going the other way. I said to the driver, "It really hurts me to hear those sounds. Someone is always in those ambulances crushed, or ill, or dying."

When we got to the house, I told him to go ahead and leave, that I would call another cab from there. Mick's house is off the highway a bit. It looked rather dark. I knocked on the door and peeped in the window, but I could hear no sounds. Then it hit me, "That was my friend in that ambulance." I ran back to the highway, trying to hail a cab. No one was stopping. Then one went by me, stopped about a block away, and turned around in the street to come for me. I told him to take me back to the International Hotel. As we drove, I told him my story of sadness and about the ambulance. Suddenly he handed me a telephone. He had dialed the hospital. "Lady, I'm the only cab in Vegas with a telephone. They call me the 'character' here in town." He had the wrong number. "Never mind, mister, I'll call from upstairs." He came back with the telephone. This time he had the right number.

"Sir, did your ambulance arrive a few moments ago with a lady?"

"Hold on." I could hear him ask. "What was that lady's name we just brought in?" Then he said to me, "We admitted a Mrs. Thompson."

"That was Mick all right. Drive on, mister, to the hospital." He just made the driveway circle in front of the hotel and headed out again.

I went to her bedside. "Mick, you can't lose me, can you? Wherever you go, I find you again."

"You sure do, honey." The nurse asked, "Do you want to sign for her clothes? Are you her sister?"

"Not the real sister, but we call each other that. Who am I, Mick?"

"Pearlie Mae." Was that a small tear trickling from her right eye? I wiped it away. Those eyes looked up at me. Then, "You're so pretty," she said.

"And so are you, Mick." She smiled. What was she doing? She gave a startled look, first showing deep concern (this I could never forget). Her eyes flashed left and right. "What's wrong, Mick?" She didn't answer at first. Then it came, "I thought I heard something."

"Remember, Mick, God is selling, are you still buying?"

"I'm buying," she said.

The nurse looked around the curtain to see the lady sitting on the next bed. Was that a black eye she had? "Do you mind," the nursed asked, "if your neighbor smokes?" Mick's little head shook a quiet "no." But she spoke. "I don't smoke anymore."

Another tear came from that right eye. I turned to the nurse and said, "I'm leaving. I must let her rest. Could I have a cloth to wipe her face before I go?" The nurse sent a fellow in who started wiping her forehead. I told him, "No, honey, the tear. Wipe away that tear."

"Mick, I'll see you tomorrow. You can't lose me. Wherever you go, I'll find you."

Did she speak? "What did you say, Mick?" I moved back to her, on the left side of her bed this time. "I'll wake up tomorrow," she said softly. Her eyes were softer, not frightened anymore. I patted her hand. "You bet you will, honey. Tomorrow and tomorrow and tomorrow."

June 24, 1970

Mr. Walter, my stepfather, died yesterday. That's what they said anyway, but they were wrong. Mr. Walter really died when Mama passed away July 18, 1969. I watched him look down into that hole, asking no one but everyone, "You mean I won't see her anymore?" Then, "Can I look once more?" It was over then.

The terrible sickness set in. Either he never knew or he refused to recognize it. He accepted it as something else. While we whispered about it, feeling that to tell him would surely be a disaster, he kept denying. Hurt, grief, and shock overruled every pain.

The grief was heavy on Mr. Walter. He had his bad days and his better days. But that lady, Mama, had set him pretty deep, never to be forgotten. They say he sometimes sat outside the house and cried, not even going inside. Forty years is a long time. Often he seemed to be shocked at how humanity could be, poor dear.

Mr. Walter, rest, dear soul. Right—wrong—grief—shock—hurt—pain. Recognize or deny. No or not no. It's all good now.

Will your restless spirit look for her, your wish fulfilled, your hearts joined in love? Your house is warm, and the landlord takes no rent.

You were my last link to Mama. So far, a year almost, no tears. A few small ones maybe, but not that ocean that normally flows at a loss. Suddenly, the stream is filling up. To-night I heard the news. Tomorrow I must look on your face. Something tells me then my tears will flow like a river. For you and Mama, the material good-bye. Why should I weep for her over you?

The house will be sold July 1. No one is home anymore. My brothers and sisters are in the city, but no one is home anymore. Do you know Charlie, the man who used to live on the third floor? He never moved farther than across the street. He died in April. Papa's brother, Uncle Frank, died this year too. And here we sit, the kids, and nobody's home.

It's strange, but as I write, the river has stopped building. I shall weep no more, for I know that someone is home after all. Here we sit, the four of us, one boy, three girls, and God will watch over. He will open the Main House. Our house on earth was never large enough. Our new one will be, you must know. There are more occupants to come. Until then, here we children shall sit and wait—

in grief
in hurt
in remorse
in shame
in pity.

But older
wiser
with more compassion
more understanding
more love—

And the house will grow larger, and we can all come home again. And the landlord will live with us.

Too Much in a Name

I had to go to Washington for the funeral of Mr. Walter, my stepfather. I chose to go by train. It took a lot of phoning and begging to get a ticket reserved. That seems funny to me with business so bad on the railroads. You really have to beg to ride the train. They insisted that I be there at 7:00 A.M.

E.B. escorted me into the station. I said, "E.B., the window for parlor cars is around here."

"No, Pearl, this way. I remember."

"E.B., I know, because I've come in here lots of times to pick up these tickets." Well, as it turned out, I had the right place okay, but the window was closed, so I ended up going around to two other windows that had a light. A handful of people were there. I asked one of the clerks, "Sir, which window is for parlor cars?"

"Around the corner, lady. They open at 7:15." So I went back around the corner. It was still closed, but I spotted a female in there chitchatting away with someone else. I pecked on the window to draw attention. "Will you be opening soon?" Her answer was absolutely beautiful—"No one is here."

"Well, I want to pick up my tickets. They're reserved."

Then she gave that wonderful answer again, "No one is here." I mumbled something to myself like, "Pearl, you're talking to no one." Then the shade raised a little higher. The lady had come over. She was chewing on something, probably her cud. She said, "We don't open today at all. Go back around the corner."

"Lady, I was there before."

She thought a minute and finally said, "Well, go back and see the boss."

"Well, who is he and where is he?"

"Just go back." I decided to try again. "Lady, please, all I want to do is to ask for two tickets made in the name of Pearl Bailey for Washington, D.C."

"You Pearl Bailey?—You sure?" I nodded. She said, "Let me go see what's wrong." I said, "Lady, that's not necessary, I just want . . ." BAM! She was gone. I stepped around to the front again and she had arrived there before me. In a split second, every clerk had been stirred up. Folks were running around in all directions. The people now in line waiting for tickets were completely ignored. And the lady who a moment ago had said she wasn't there at all was in the center of it like a queen bee.

At Last, for Them All

I went from the train to the hotel to change clothes. I put on a black dress and that same veil that I had worn now three times in one year. I hadn't really wept for Mama or the others, not the ocean that I thought would come. Now we were going to bury Mr. Walter.

When I got to the church, the people were standing on the sidewalk waiting to be ushered in, two by two. I walked past them up the stairs. No one stopped me. The rest of the family had already gone in. Someone in the line waved a "Hello, Pearl." I did not respond. That was not the time to do so. It was a large church. The moment I stepped inside the door I saw, way up front, the casket. I did what probably was a childish thing and a funny thing as I think about it now. I clenched my fists and threw them down at my sides like a person would in disgust. It was like a little child saying, "Oh boy, here it is again." Against the back wall of the sanctuary, I found a bench and sat down. I sat staring at that casket way up front, and I felt the ocean starting to build. Then, in one of the pews in front of me, I saw a nice-looking young man with glasses on. I recognized him as my nephew, whom we all called "Brother." I walked over and slipped in beside him. Without saying a word, he clasped my hand tightly. The services started. Time and again, Brother squeezed my hand. It was as if he wanted to squeeze back his emotion. Once I turned to him and whispered, "Brother, he was a good person."

"I know, Aunt Dick, that's why I'm here." Near the end of the service, an usher sat down behind me and said, "The family will open the casket for you before we leave for the cemetery." The viewing had been the day before. I'm sure the family thought that it would be a wonderful favor to let me see Mr. Walter. He had been so fond of me, always calling me his baby. In the midst of all of the agony and grief that my family had suffered, I realized that this was a very unselfish gesture. I shook my head, no, no more grief or pain. I knew that it would be rough enough for them when they had to go back home and he would not be there. Two men moved toward the casket, which was on rollers. I got out of my seat and walked to the front of the church and looked at that box. For a moment, everyone was in it—Papa, Mama, Mr. Walter, Mickey. I cried out. I could hear myself—that one tortured sound for them all.

The box started to move on its rollers. I put my hand on it and helped the men to push. I guess. A nurse came near me. I didn't need help, so I moved her hand away. All I could do was keep walking with my hand on the box. The reverend said, somewhere behind me, "That's love." As I went down the aisle toward the front doors of the church, all I could think was, "You bet it is, sir, you bet it is."

Brother and I went to the grave. Fanny, Mr. Walter's sister, gave me the crank to the casket. "Please, Fanny, I don't want it. He's not in there." Spiritually, all of my family, living and dead, were close around me. They were keeping me warm with their love. For a time there, it seemed that no one really was gone. Thinking about this later one day in my kitchen in New York, I said to E.B., "I wonder how it feels to die? I wonder where they all go?" Such a child-thing to say, huh?

I spent some time back at the house with all the members of the family, and I was never really alone until I got back to New York again. There, I found a chance to wander around, let my thoughts come to lead me into emotion. By that time, I was ready.

Spots

There's a spot of earth I call Mama,
And another one called Papa,
And spots called Mickey and Mr. Walter.

One day I planted flowers
In each spot.

There is a star up there I call Mama,
And one for Papa, and stars for
Celia, and Don, and Mr. Walter,

And . . .
Do I still know each face?

There's a spot in my heart.
I wonder, sometimes,
Why it aches so.

The fullness, the loneliness,

and the fright . . .

Emotions in Song

To perform a song successfully, the singer must feel powerful emotions about the song, particularly its lyrics—and the audience must catch that feeling too. Sometimes in my act I do a medley of songs from the forties. At first I thought this music might be a little too old. When I began to relearn the lyrics, however, and when I tried these songs on the stage, I realized that they are not too old at all. They are very warm songs. I feel them very strongly because I have lived them. I am doing more than a recitation of words to music. I am doing my life. As I sing, those lyrics take me back to good and bad moments associated with places, conversations, people, all kinds of good and bad memories. As I sing, I feel again the pain and the forgiveness. I remember the values received or given. The complete picture comes into focus, so that my mind and heart can enjoy the same understanding.

And so I sing, pouring forth my insides. Others who have lived fully will respond. If I help them to recall happier times, let them laugh. If they remember sad times, let them cry. If I sing of love, let that audience become aware of itself through my awareness of life.

The Eye of the Beholder

When you know what music a person understands and likes, you know something important about him. When anyone asks Louis Armstrong what jazz is, he always says, "If you have to ask, then you'll never know."

I always notice the kind of music that the kids like at any given time. When rock got started, it was pretty sloppy music, but lately the kids have become more skillful in the business of composing and playing in a disciplined way. Still, something bothers me about their music of today. It shows a deep sadness in the kids. The troubled situations of the world have had an effect. When I hear their music, I wonder, do the children see the roses bloom? Do they any longer notice the beauty of a raindrop? Their tones and their lyrics are so sad. In King Arthur's day, the troubadours went around singing messages, political and otherwise. Isn't that it now? Our children are singing rightly sad songs. When will their music show laughter again? To write and sing songs of negativism is comparatively easy. Who needs a real tune for that? The children are singing from their hearts these days, and are composing in the key of "help us."

Pity

She looked so lonely. I guessed her to be about fifteen, sitting on the beach at Tahoe, wearing slacks and a blouse top, throwing sand in the edge of the water to make a game for herself. Other teenagers passed by from time to time, laughing and giggling their happiness. They did not seem to see the girl. Slowly, she arose—huge, huge she was. She turned and walked slowly down the beach. A lady, probably her mother, stood, brushed the sand from her clothes, and walked slowly behind.

Satchmo

It's a pleasant feeling to feel proud of another person. That's how I feel about Louis Armstrong. He is a very great artist and a fine man. Now, of course, he is not necessarily the greatest singer in the world, but when you hear him it sounds as if he is hitting every other harmonic note that goes with the melody line he is following. It's all there, the whole chord—complete. He is interested and thrilled that the audience feels his singing, his entertainment, his heart, his message for them—"I love you very much and I love what I'm doing to make you enjoy me." He will be sad if ever people feel left out of his joy. He is a love.

The Little Ones

I was walking up Madison Avenue when I saw the hearse on a side street. Automatically, I was drawn near. The door of the hearse was open and the pallbearers came out of the church. I wandered to the side and leaned against a tree, watching. Behind the hearse there was one car. The people inside watched the box with the American flag draped over it.

I walked over to the car, leaned down to the window and

said, "Excuse me, you're a part of that casket, aren't you?" There were six youngsters in the car. One of them answered, "Yes." Then the girl by the window in the back seat (eyes so red) said, "He was my boyfriend."

I said, "Sweetheart, I'm not leaning in here to meddle. Only two weeks ago I too followed a car like that. And in eleven months, I've followed the hearse three times. He is not in there, dear. His soul has gone. Please accept what God wills and take it as easily as you can. He is not there. He has found peace." She smiled warmly and so did the others. Quietly I left, then turned back to look as they were bringing the flowers out.

Then a school bus turned the corner, with little heads peeping out. They were between six and eight years old, and all thirty of them were screaming. When they saw the hearse, they began a song, "Somebody's dead, somebody's dead." There was a beauty in it because it was so innocent, and yet it was sad because I knew this carload of teenagers could hear the chant.

I stepped over to the bus. Traffic was stopped anyway because the bus was unloading the kids. I saw a lady there who was one of the teachers, I guess. She didn't say a word to these kids. Why not? Couldn't she see and hear what was going on? Their voices were penetrating. I looked up at those darling faces and motioned with my finger to my lips, "Be quiet now." I spoke to a couple of children and said, "The people in the car will hear you, and they're very sad now." The kids stopped and their eyes grew big. One little boy said, "Who's dead, lady?"

"A soldier," I answered. Their faces began to look sad and then even sadder. All the children grew silent. I walked away from the bus and waved my hand at them and they waved back. I watched them close the door of the hearse, and traffic moved on.

Despair

A feeling of being the last car
On a slow train
Going uphill.

I know we'll go down faster
But I will still be last
So why rush?

Why rush to push
The others down—
And down to where?

Meeting

The man walked into the dark TV booth, was introduced, sat down, then arose and came around to the chair next to me and sat down there. "I have something in mind for you," he said. I looked closely at this man. It was dark in there. I said, "Mr. Merrick, I have heard about you. If I ever return to the Broadway stage, I'd be happy to return for you because I know you'll do a show right." He said, "You'll hear from me." That was in June of 1966 as we were taping a show for *What's My Line?*

In September or October we reached an agreement. I got the news from my manager, Stan, in London. No one knew about this plan, not even my agency. Actually there were only four people who knew it, Merrick, Louie, Stan, and myself. It turned out to be one of the best-kept secrets in show business. Much later, David told me that after we spoke he had had second thoughts about sharing such a secret with me so early. He had no idea that a woman could keep a secret that way.

I received the script in March of 1967 in Houston. I was working at the Cork Club, but I took the necessary forty minutes to race through the script. There was no doubt in my mind that I could be Dolly. I also knew without a doubt who else should be in the play. I called my manager immediately and said, "There's only one person in the world who could be Vandergelder—Cab Calloway." He spoke with Merrick and they began looking for Cab, but couldn't get in touch with him. I stuck with it and finally he was found.

We started *Dolly* in September of 1967 in New York far away from my California home. The legitimate theater had not claimed me since 1954. Okay, sure, I had done vaudeville, TV, and so on, but I hadn't had anything that could be classified as an extended run. As the time for the opening drew near, I would sit in the backyard by the pool in California and discuss the implications of a long-term engagement with Louie. It bothered me then to think that I might be separated from my family for a very long time. Louie said that his work was flexible, he could locate on one coast as well as the other, and why didn't we all move to New York for a time. As it turned out later he couldn't really make the move, and there were many times when both he and I wished that we had worked it out somehow.

Sometimes I used to walk down from the St. James

Theatre to the pier. I would sit and look at the boats with my feet hanging over the edge. I sat and looked into that water, and I felt the sun. I saw people getting on and going up and down the river to see the Statue of Liberty, and the water gave me its show, dancing and glistening. The boat gave me its own kind of show, opening its jaws to swallow humanity trudging up the gangplank. Then it would turn and plow through the water with people waving at nothing, on their way around Manhattan or to Europe. I participated in their little show, waving farewell to people I didn't know. I enjoyed the excitement that others felt, but I was a little sad to feel that I had no time, no possibility, of getting on that boat.

Professional Loneliness

I walked through the park. Two men passed me and one turned back and spoke, "I know you, lady." He was very strong-looking with a good face. He said, "I'm an athlete. Baseball."

"What baseball, mister?" I'm the mascot for the Mets and I know lots of players by now. "Which team is yours?"

He said, "Oh, I go back."

"Then go back, mister, go back to headphones if you have to. That's when I started listening to baseball."

Then he told me a story.

"Well, Jackie Robinson, myself, and a few others, we started it off. I'm really one of the first. Sam Jethro. I was with the Boston Braves and St. Louis." He was on his way to Japan, after having just been to Spain. I asked him how he felt leaving the game after thirteen or fourteen years. Did he miss it? He said, "I hardly look at a game now. I'm glad I learned something else to do. Most of all, I like the feeling of being able to live like other people. It's wonderful. I've learned to eat and sleep normally and enjoy my family. Being a normal human being is fun, you know."

He was right. I know that he is right because I very seldom get to live like a normal person, and I do miss it. People in certain professions have pressures that normal working people don't have. There is a loneliness in it. I, for one, keep searching for a corner.

Doctors have this problem. There is that standard joke, "Oh, you're a doctor. Well, I've got a pain right here." The doctors laugh, but it really isn't quite as funny to them. No one seems to want to realize that a doctor is human and needs to be treated as just a person sometimes. His professional position comes into every casual conversation. I know a doctor whose relatives call him coast-to-coast as if they just couldn't find another physician anyplace.

The old country docs used to take chickens or flour in payment. Even relatives try to give a country doc something to help him along. That's better than now in a way. Today, when a doctor does something for a relative, the doctor gets nothing except maybe a Sunday dinner with more questions.

The same sort of thing happens to some of us in the theater. People don't know how lonely they make us sometimes. "Come on over to our house and relax. Forget about your business. We'll just have a great time. We have a piano and we could sing a few songs. We would love to have you. . . ."

Making Friends with Loneliness

After the long run in *Hello, Dolly!* and going on the road with the show, I got physically tired, almost to the point of dying. So the doctors say. And I know it was true. Thinking back, I realize that a lot of people couldn't believe that I could get weary. Maybe that's because always if I had one ounce of energy left, I spent it freely and completely. Finally, the doctors said, "No more," and I had to leave the show in Houston.

Long before that business, however, I developed habits of stillness and meditation. Time and again, people have become alarmed to see me quiet, my face without a smile. I learned about meditation in the hospital. It is a matter of making friends with loneliness.

You start to gather up all your wheat and leave the chaff behind. For a while, they gave me mild sedation to force my muscles and my mind to relax. It wasn't the kind of sedative that puts you out of it or makes you think you are something else. This led me to contemplation.

When I came back out of that loneliness into life situations, I was more ready to accept things better than before. I could see things for their value. After the extended quietness there was a spiritual strength, an ability to approach things and do more about them than before.

I had reached a point where the doctors were discussing whether I would make it or not. Afterward, it really shook me to think that I had almost taken that one step beyond the things that the world can do for you. Now, when I see a fellow man making my mistakes, I want to take his shoulder and just shake him and say, "It isn't worth it. It will do to you what it has done to me."

I guess I've always known that I'm an emotional person.

Many times people have said to me something that really galls me, "Pearl, you must rise above this problem. Don't let it get you so emotional." Every time I feel that statement coming, I just think, oh, please don't say it. Once I lashed back. "Rise above what? I don't want to rise above my fellow man, above concern for him. I don't want to rise above the earth, I want to be on it and in it."

There was a time, if I'm going to be honest, when personal relationships hit me so deeply that I could have gone under. In fact, I feel things just as strongly now. But there is something else, something that started with loneliness and went beyond it—something that started with worry and arrived at meditation.

The View from the Hospital

Although I had been in there for a while, no one had come to visit me and no one had called to ask how I was. Sure, I said it didn't matter, but it did matter to me. I can tell you honestly now it mattered because I really wanted that love, that concern. I don't care about getting attention in and of itself, but I do like to know that people care. I was just sure that they cared, but I wanted to know that it was really true. No one came and no one called.

Dr. Rizzo used to come in each morning. I'd give him a big smile and he'd return it. Somehow it crept out. "Well, Doc, I haven't heard from anyone yet." We both smiled. I know that inside it mattered to him too, just as it mattered to me. It hurt him in a way because it was hurting me. Both of us were saying that it didn't really matter. The main thing was that I get some rest and so on. Truly, it was the hardest part of being in the hospital—the absence of loved ones.

Had it been known publicly that I was in the hospital, there would have been flowers and notes all over the place. Many of them from people I didn't even know. Still, there were plenty of people I worked with who knew I was in the hospital and hadn't done a thing. I longed to smell the sweet scent of "How are you?"

One night the whole thing closed in on me and I took the courage to protect myself from these feelings. I knew that I had to get up and go back to the stage, back to the responsibilities that awaited me. Going back, I felt intense love, a realization of how good it was to be there again. Yes, even the jealousies between people seemed to have a useful meaning.

The whole thing was another step in my growing up and learning more about people. It was interesting for me to watch show business people afraid to love, afraid to become fully human beings—for fear of losing what? Themselves? Or was it each other? Their only support was gained from holding on to each other's alter egos. These people, I could see clearly now, were screwing each other and no one was getting laid. Their code was, "we stand firm in our belief that to become human would destroy us." I knew that they were already lonely and destroyed. No one could possibly continue for a long time to trust these people, or to love them fully, because they were so terribly sad. They were miserably lonely. What a price to pay. All at once, the price that I had paid did not seem so high. My price only required more giving.

Fifteen Days

I lay flat on my back—twenty pounds of traction. Tired. Terribly tired. I asked myself, "How long can I keep it up?" I'm not sick, but I will be. Why can't they just let me rest a bit. I'm not trying to ignore my work or my responsibility. I'm not just dismayed by the trials and tribulations of life. I had to leave the show to rest, and I'm going back. I repeat it again so everyone can hear. Dearhearts, when I cannot give all to the people who come to see me, then I would rather not be there at all. I cannot stand to cheat on an audience.

Loneliness and Despair

Anthony Quinn, a fine man and a wonderful actor, brought his wife and a few friends backstage to see me after a performance of *Dolly* in New York. After a few minutes we began to discuss life and the progress we had made since the old days. We have known each other for years and years. After a while, he started to leave and then stepped back into the room. I asked simply, "Tony, did I do the job all right?" He said, "You're something like myself. You give life as you see it—you give a power from within." Then he stopped to write down a quotation for me (whether it was his or someone else's I don't know) :

You will wander on and on with your ill-concealed yearning. And in all your loneliness you will not find the one friend who will open to thee the kingdom in your own breast.

Magnificent. For all our great social activity in the theater, we find such a loneliness. All the world thinks we are so terribly brave and terribly alive. There is that about us to a degree. Yet, on this particular night that Tony Quinn gave me the quotation, I had been away from my family for a long time. They were working and studying in California while I worked in New York.

I knew that I was going to have to go home to the loneliness of that apartment. I would have coffee at my kitchen table and then start thinking about going to bed.

The bedrooms in my apartment were upstairs. Since I was a child I have always liked the idea of upstairs and downstairs. I like the feeling of saying, as Mama always did, "Go upstairs and go to bed."

Suddenly, sitting at the kitchen table, I realized I couldn't go upstairs to bed anymore. I was alone and it didn't make any sense. Oh, I had love. My goodness, I couldn't have received any more love each night from the people in my audiences. I received loving every day too. People who loved me and people whom I loved. So what was the matter with me? Fantastic!

I kept the radio in the living room on all the time at a crazy FM station, WPIX—that beautiful music. The disc jockeys hardly say a word. Finally, I made my bed on the floor between the record player and the sofa. It became a regular habit with me. Sometimes, for variation, I would doze on the sofa, and morning would find me there. It went on for months. I completely ignored this immense apartment full of rooms. Each night, after *Dolly*, I would just get a sheet and a blanket and make the grandest bed in the world right under that music.

The different sounds brought various memories. Sometimes, many times, dear world, the music brought such beautiful memories that my heart would seem to break. I wanted those memories to come back, exist again at that very moment. I wanted to laugh and smile and just have someone to look at.

Sometimes I would get up and make more coffee. While I was sitting there drinking it I would smile and think, "Isn't this something. What if those audiences could see me now. They must think that after the curtain goes down on all that glamour at the St. James Theatre, I go out to some grand place and have a wonderful time." Actually, I just sat there sometimes and felt very sorry for myself. It was, if you please, a kind of meditation, and meditation is something that I've always valued. There's a limit to how much solitude I can take, though. There I sat and thought, "Thanks a lot. Big lady, huh! And here you sit. It's not that you don't know people. You could have invited people over." What it really came down to was that I wanted my children and my husband. I wanted them there with me even if they were all sound asleep.

Many times Lou would call and say, "Honey, it's so lonely here." And I'd say, "It's lonely here too." Yeh, Lou says he's lonely. But I found myself feeling envious of him. He could, after all, walk in and look at the children if he wanted to. And the next morning at breakfast, he would find that Lucille had put good things on the table and the children would be there waiting.

After the phone call, I would just want desperately to see someone to have that cup of coffee with. If I had had my way in the beginning, all nine rooms of the apartment would have been filled with family and friends. When we saw that *Dolly* was going to run a long time, I had arranged for all my family to join me. But then, after I signed the lease, plans had changed.

I decided that what I really needed was something to help remind me of that house in California, to make me feel the presence of my loved ones in some way. So I sent for some of the furniture out of the house, mainly the living-room things. I really loved that living room, because I had decorated it myself, mixing all the colors and doing the painting. I like colors anyway. Sometimes I paint on plain tablet paper—things that would make Rembrandt turn over. Michelangelo would never lie on his back again.

Okay, so the furniture helped a little. Turn off the coffee-pot, pick up the big old brown cup, and go back to the living room where my music is. Then I would sit down on the sofa with my coffee on the table and go into a sort of fantasy world, entertaining everyone. I would sit there many times in that land and choke on sheer loneliness.

I found I could be aware of both the fantasyland and the real land at the same time, comparing them. While in the faraway world, I was ever-present in the near one. The near world existed and it was true. Nevertheless, in my faraway world, there were people there, the pulse of living. Their love was in the room because they wanted it there. But as a mature adult being I had to know I was alone. As a spiritual being, I knew that I had God.

On the night when Tony Quinn gave me the quotation it hit me very hard. I went through my ritual, getting my coffee, going into the living-room. ". . . you will not find one friend to open the kingdom in your breast." That was how it went, right? Somehow I began to realize that even when things were temporarily unhappy, God and truth remained there always. They fill not one spot at one time, but every corner of every room and every heart. Having realized that, I could lie down on my little pallet on the floor and wake up the next day knowing that I would see humanity again—that I would smile and come back to life. I knew that I had one perfectly dependable Great Companion.

Sanctuary

I wish that sometime you could stand on an empty stage in an empty theater with only the work light on. It is one of the loneliest-looking things in the world, one of the most beautiful, awesome and frightening too. I make it a point sometimes to go in and see the theater empty. Sometimes, having stood there for a while, I find I want to stay. If the theater had permitted it, I would have stayed all night.

Sometimes I would go to work very early, step out on the stage and say to myself, "Yes, this is it. This is what I wanted to do as a little girl." Then I would walk across the stage, stop, look up, and remember the people. In my imagination, I could see their faces and hear their laughter. I would think, yes, I have something to give and thank God it gives me back so much. I would look at the rows of empty seats and remember that I had had the privilege of seeing them full of happy people. I also realized the overwhelming thrill of having the people forget all about their seats to stand and cheer, as they did so often in *Hello, Dolly!*

Then I would just stand and savor the fullness, the loneliness, and the fright. Taken altogether, the experience never failed to be comforting, like religion in a rare form.

The measure

of its contents . . .

Begging for Breath

I had flown to New York on Tuesday, and then hurried back to *Dolly* on the road. I was supposed to return to New York again on Wednesday night to attend to more business. Jack Schlissel called and said, "Don't come, because you looked tired today while I was talking with you." Lord, Jack is a hard-driving man, so I had to heed that message. It was a kind and thoughtful expression from him. Looking back on it now, I think that he may have saved my life.

Wednesday after the matinee, I came out of the theater for dinner feeling extremely tired. Autograph seekers were there waiting for me. I said, "Please forgive me today, I don't feel well." Then the usual routine started, "Oh, please, just one." They wanted me to answer, to understand, to shake hands. I could feel weariness overtaking me completely. I felt that all I could do was smile and keep moving. One man was very persistent. It seems there is always one like him. On top of everything else, he was trying to be a comedian of sorts. Don't you love people with humor as you are begging for one more breath? I found myself thinking of Zorba the Greek—take the raiment, jewels and all, but let me suck in one more breath. Finally a youthful voice came from a teenage girl, "Mister, can't you see she's tired?" Bless her. Bless her heart. Looking around, I caught her face and thanked her. Then, having stopped, I realized I would have to sign the autograph anyway. I did it quickly and began to move again.

I heard the sound of footsteps behind me. There were two young beautiful children following with sad looks on their faces. I remember thinking at the time that maybe they pitied both the man and me. Roz and I had decided to go to a Japanese restaurant nearby. The boy and girl remained behind us. Finally I turned, and on an impulse, invited them to have a cup of tea with us. Once we were seated, I figured why not have them for the whole dinner? They were very polite, Spanish they said. The boy excused himself and called his mother. He was very excited and wanted to invite me to his home. Temporarily I took strength from the love of these children. But soon that terrible heaviness in my chest came back. Where was my breath going?

I heard myself saying, "Please, children, will you walk me back to the theater?" That is unusual for me, but I was thinking of that board, that faithful board or the faithful floor in my dressing room where I often try to catch a nap. My breath was definitely going away. "Good-bye, children."

As I passed the doorman, I asked him to call a doctor—not urgent—just where was my breath going?—Harder to find—slower and heavier—

Word got to Norman of the theater staff. He came in. "What can I do, Miss Bailey?"

"Nothing dear. I just—want to rest." He stepped out. Did I hear him calling for emergency? For oxygen? Who were the people coming in? I think I was slipping out of consciousness. Policemen came storming into the room. I had a strange feeling of being arrested. I said something like, "Mama, we're going to jail." A navy doctor appeared, a very nice man, and gave me some nitroglycerin. "You should go to the hospital."

"But the show, what about . . ." More sirens and policemen. Finally a stretcher. "Lady, you really should go, and now."

"Will you get me back in time for the show?"

"Oh, yes. This is really just a precaution." Then I was on the stretcher and on my way out. Did I see Laverne's face, sad as always? No, perhaps not.

Later I found out that the hospital was practically across the street. I must have looked silly going over there on a stretcher. By now, all of my sensations were mixed up. In my memory I have flashes of those frenzied minutes before I went to the hospital. Our assistant to the assistant stage manager, a man I call Gentle Sam, was actually screaming his fanny off, "Let Miss Bailey out. Take care of her. She's ill." In a way, I think Gentle Sam was in worse shape than I was. At one point, he and the doctor got into it hot and heavy.

Once in the hospital, the decision was that I had to remain there. No evening performance. Turmoil reigned. They made calls to my New York doctor. Then they sent big wheels to my room, specialists. They were men of great patience. With all of this going on, I got up from there and I said, "Give me my coat." Nobody made a move but Gentle Sam. He knew that I was leaving. One of the doctors said, "If you leave here, it's as good as suicide. You need a night's rest, and we'll look at you again in the morning." My sister Eura appeared. She had heard about the whole thing on the radio. Then Virgie, my other sister, arrived. And Mr. Kusell, the company manager. After that, Cab Calloway, Roz, and my faithful friend, E.B. Meanwhile, Louie was frantic on the phone trying to get information.

As more people arrived, it came to me that I did not have the strength to get across the street to the stage. It just wasn't there.

On Saturday night, I finally begged my way out of Jefferson Memorial Hospital. Some of the people who had treated me followed me over there and caught the show. I performed, loved, packed, and left for Detroit, where a number of people had heard I was dead.

Detour Failure

Many people get to a detour in the road and think that's the end of the road entirely. They toss it in, give up. Folks, there's always an arrow there. It shows where the detour goes, and if you follow, you'll eventually get back on your course. Going a bit out of the way shouldn't disturb you. Even backing up sometimes is necessary. There's an art in knowing when to back up and when to detour. The essential thing is the faith that you will make it eventually. The alternative is plunging off the bridge that isn't there.

False Death

Long ago, a girl of eleven, I realized that I had to die at forty—not a real physical death, but the death of material concern. When forty came, I still felt the same about this, so awaited my appointment with false death. Then, when I was forty-one, playing on the stage at the Tivoli, in Chicago, the change came. After our show, there was an onstage gathering and party for all the cast. Just as the gaiety was starting, something came to me. I arose, walked up the stairs, and sat in the chair by the door of my dressing room —still and quiet. In that moment, my false death came. I was ready to give myself up to it, ready to accept the voice that must be listened to. That was eleven years ago, and the change has been permanent.

I hear the voice
That must be listened to—
It speaks each day.
What work the Master picks
I must do
And God so will—
Will do.

Show-business Fear

Show-business fear is the fear of falling from high places. It is a possessive fear that seems to me a show of greed or feelings of inferiority. Any performer who is fully confident of his talent, God-given, and who places a high value on it for its own sake, cannot fear so much.

The worry comes in when a performer asks, "Do I really have this gift that others now seem to admire so much? Would I still get respect from others if I lost my touch?" Fear of failure anticipates self-pity. Once having had recognition and acclaim, some performers begin at once to pity themselves because someday the recognition will not be there.

It is true that as big as you are in the business, it's always possible for someone to overshadow you at any time. The only protection is faith in yourself and in your talent. I know that God gave me whatever talents I have. No matter what happens to me, I will not surrender to despair. They can take my money, my fame, but there is no way for anyone to take away the gift of talent. Even if I have no place to use it but in heaven, no one can take it away from me.

Bounce

Some of the biggest failures I ever had were successes. A man has to try in order to grow, and try again. The point is that it's the trying that does it, and not necessarily achieving what he is attempting to do.

For every failure, one grows a bit. Failure inspires some people to go on, at least that's the way it affects the greats of show business as I've observed them. Some of these people who have had bad times and still come back remind me of the doctor who had to decide what to do about his first serious mistake in medicine. He had to head for the jungle to find out how and why he had been wrong. He had to think, "Maybe I will learn something that will save ten people, or maybe a lion will eat me and end my career altogether."

Responding to temporary failure takes real skill. Think of baseball players you have observed. One misses the ball for strike three. Sixty or seventy thousand people are looking at him, not counting the possible TV audience. He can put down the bat and say, "Yes, I struck out, it just isn't my day. I can hit that ball, and next time I get to bat, I'll show what I can do." On the other hand, some athletes under the same circumstances get angry and embarrassed. They argue, throw the bat down. Really, it's not the strike three that matters to them, it is that all those people are watching.

The world tends to be cruel to a failure who knows he is a failure. We are not very good at staying with a person who is down, to help him get up again. Likewise, we are impatient with people who do an acceptable job, but not a superlative job of anything. I have tried to make my own children think differently. I have told them, "Everyone cannot be a hundred percenter. You may not be the best at what you try, but you can try harder than anyone else." I have taught them that if they try very hard, they cannot really fail at anything.

Joe E. Lewis is one of the most loved men in the theatrical world (a jovial Santa Claus, with or without his bag). He's been very ill lately. One thing everybody said about Lewis was that he has always had the determination to try and try again. So when he got well, they came from every part of the country to pay tribute to a man who always had the courage to carry on. Sitting on the dais was Harry Richman, another real trouper. Harry is advancing in age, but nevertheless, he got up and did his best, singing "Birth of the Blues," a wonderful song that he introduced years and years ago. His voice is, in a sense, gone, yet he did the song beautifully, with all the movements and gestures. I really wept for the class of it all. These men have something the world needs.

As I write this, Joe Louis is staying for a while in a hospital to rest. He is the greatest of all the champions to me. Every now and then, he comes out and you see him. The remarkable thing is that with all of the bad fortune he has had, you never hear him complain. He is a true champion,

trying to make the best of everything. To my way of thinking, the only people who really are sick are those who are
no longer willing to try.

Louis Armstrong hadn't worked for two years. He had
been quite sick. Then, recently he came back to Vegas to
work the International with me. What a thrill to see that
energy and dedication. He played that horn and sang with
much love. It seemed that he had never been happier. A new
life at seventy.

For performers who bounce back, some of the motive is
that desire for the recognition and love that audiences give.
Part of it is sheer personal dedication. In any case, after a
defeat or a long absence, it takes courage to go back on the
stage. I have had to do this more than once, and I know.

Brother

After two operations, at fifty-eight
Sitting upstairs in his house,
Still with those crutches,
Bill tried to cope with ten children,
Screaming downstairs to them,
None answering or understanding.

"Dick" (he called me that), "What now?"

Dear Brother, I do not know.
It will take all you can give,
And all you can take,
And maybe more.

God loves you, who stood
So grandly on that stage.
There is a way;
There is hope yet. Hold on.
Pay the full debt,
For there is time to live.

Jail Fear

I had never been inside a jail. Even for a visitor, there is a
shock about the first time. A steel gate clanging open and
shut. I sat in a room until they called my name. A policeman
escorted me upstairs, past more bars, and finally to the pris-
oner, my friend, behind a steel door. He talked to me on the
telephone, his face showing great strain. "Get me out, get
me out!" Screaming. He couldn't even tell me his story.

Touched by Fire

At Lake Tahoe, Lou and I walked three to five miles a day
through the forest. We went single file all the way, each one
enjoying the experience in his own manner. I saw those
beautiful trees making love to the sky, and I felt I was seeing what life was really all about.

I began to think of those trees as people, some standing
very tall and some quite short, yet all there in their glory, as
if to say, "I am a part of it, and how good is God."

Some of the trees had been touched by a forest fire. There

were stumps and there were those trees that had been almost, but not quite, completely destroyed. Most were brown and beginning to decay. I thought of those tall but lifeless trees as faithful, holding themselves up as if in hope that, protected from further harm, they might survive their condition. We could all take a lesson from that.

The nubby stumps didn't take away from the beauty of the forest. They were sad to see, of course, but they seemed a useful reminder of what man's destructiveness can do. The burned limbs and stumps for me symbolized hope in the face of difficulty—the will to live and replace life even after devastation.

I asked myself, "Have you been touched by fire?" Yes, of course, we all have been touched by fire. We have been touched by ice too. They both can kill; and yet both can protect life.

Doodle

Something wild has been happening lately. Now that I have an office in New York, I've been doodling while I talk with staff and acquaintances. I'm not an artist (always terrible in art at school, where even an apple ended up square). Nevertheless, I have found myself drawing something—the same thing over and over again. I've been swinging the pencil back and forth into the same lines. Once with a whole page of this in front of me, I stopped to ask myself what these figures were. All I could imagine was that they looked exactly like cups, but why?

Then a voice came to me, "The cup is the cup of life. It is meant to drink from. Fill it, lady, and learn to temper yourself as you drink from it. Drink so much and no more. Accept the measure of its contents and find contentment."

Self-control: What Is It?

Is self-control exactly the same as self-discipline? Can we say that a person has self-control if he seems serene, but harbors a smoldering volcano of resentment underneath? If the volcano is there is it not God-given like all parts of us, good and bad?

Through self-discipline, one can learn to avoid being around situations which require self-control. Does it really make sense to talk about self-discipline and self-control if what you are actually doing is walking away? I know a man whose presence controls others better than he controls himself. He has a silence, a warmth, an agreeability. He can make you look like a perfect ass if you go any other way. He maintains his self-control by separating himself from humanity in a way. If he became a part of humanity, could he have that self-control? I say if you can live in this world, partake of it, get the hurts, the insults, and everything—and still control yourself—then you honestly do have self-control. On the other hand, if you never let the world touch you, but hold it at arm's length, or move away from it, then that is not necessarily self-control. It is a necessary self-discipline in the absence of self-control. I am looking for the kind of selfhood that will allow me to draw near to the best and worst of human experience, do what I can, and come out still myself.

Ball Games

"Come on, Joel, let's go to a ball game. You're twenty-five years old. Enjoy life a little. You should see a game, it will add to your experience. So far, you only know about discotheques and hippyville. Do yourself a favor and join us older ones in that old-time national pastime, baseball." A speech like that had to get him. Joel was a fine young man who worked in casting for the Merrick organization.

"Okay, Pearl," he said. "You treat me to a ball game and then I'll treat you to a show." We went to see the Mets and the Giants. My amazing Mets. It was a beautiful Sunday afternoon. We sat right up front at the railing, guests of Gil Hodges. I enjoy getting up close that way. I started in the bleachers, and sometimes I even got enjoyment as a child looking through a hole in the fence. Willie Mays crossed over from the Giants' dugout to speak to us. Joel almost fainted. It was just too much for one day. Willie is really the icing on the cake. He is truly one of the greatest baseball players of all times. When they saw Willie, the people in the stands started rushing down toward the railing. They almost crushed us. The photographer was taking pictures. Willie said, "Pearl, you're from California, what are you doing on this side? You belong over there with us." I told a gorgeous fib. "Willie, I'm over here to observe you. This way I can look in your dugout and wish you guys the best." (Ho, ha, go go, Mets!)

The Mets won, and we were off to the night show. I had heard the name of it, it was one of the nude shows. Now, I've seen the Lido shows in Paris. They've been topless for a while. But I had never seen the whole thing, definitely not. When we got to the Village, we found the theater jammed with people trying to get tickets. They were elegant folks, apparently the elite.

Now when I say the show came on, I really mean that. The curtain came up and everyone was completely naked, bare. The lights were bright, like work lights. And those kids up there were working. It all seemed unnecessary in a way. This nakedness is becoming so common in the theater now that it's losing even its pioneering value for the theater. I thought about the actors up there. They obviously believe in what they are doing or want to do it for some reason. After all, how much could they be making in this tiny theater? They all looked happy enough. Yes, they showed their faces too. Their figures were quite okay. Some were a bit bony, and some a bit too much here and there. All had the right count. Some things they did seemed to me a bit too vulgar. Not new, just vulgar. They went on and on, and I began to wonder just how soon they would be off. I think that I have some sense of art, and I know that art doesn't get boring.

At intermission Joel was in stitches. He found the whole thing to be hilarious. Lots of other people were practically on the floor with laughter. To be fair, I'd have to say that others were cringing in their seats from disgust or shame or something. Some looked green, as if ill. And a few walked out. I sat there for the rest of it, all life deserves a chance. Who knows, I thought, at the end they might put on their clothes again. Salvation and hallelujah! They might have taken off their skins and rattled their bones for us. Whichever way the ball was going to bounce, if there was anything to learn, I was going to be there. I was paying the full price of being part of an audience. I found myself chewing three sticks of gum. Why did I do that?

After the show, I hit Joel playfully on his head. Clunk! "How dare you bring me here after that beautiful ball game. What is this supposed to represent? Sex? I'll tell you, son, there's more sex on the ball field when the guys scratch than in the whole of this." He said, "Pearl, it's a put-on."

I said, "I wish they'd put on something, because I'm tired of looking at their fannies."

As we left the theater, the thing that impressed me was the shuffling of feet, the heads cast downward, the peculiar silence in the crowd. No one really looked at one another. Men and women who had come in together avoided each other's gaze. Perhaps they were taken with what they had seen on the stage and now were thinking, "Oh hell, I have to go home with this."

An old friend of mine, Leonard Sillman, a gentlemen of the theater, took Joel and me to Luchow's for supper after the theater. I love that place. We talked about the show we had seen. Joel said, "Pearl, it was artistic."

"Let me tell you something," I said. "Real art brings on a wonderful, warm feeling. It gets an honest emotional response. If that had been artful—those nude bodies, sex orgies, and whatever that was supposed to be, then not one man or one woman in that audience would have been able to get up for fifteen or twenty minutes afterward. They would have been aroused. I don't think it's just that we are trained as human beings to look on that stage and remain placid. There was something missing there."

It was disappointing theater. I meant what I said to Joel. The fact is though that I'm not really sure whether it was the play that was missing something or the audience that was at fault because it was prepared not to respond.

Spontaneity

Each man works in a different way. Lou, Dodi, and E.B. are detail people. They prepare things far ahead. If Louie is going to open someplace in a week, he has every day planned. Monday he will take care of his music and his clothes. Tuesday he prepares something else, and so forth. All week long the excitement and nervousness grows. On the other hand, if I am a week away from an opening, I'm not thinking about details at all. I tend to just let things happen. Louie almost goes to pieces over this. "Honey, what about your songs and dresses?" He worries.

"Louie, I don't even know what you're worried about."

"Well, so-and-so worked that stage a year ago, and he said . . ."

"Oh, please, honey, it's going to be all right. Louie, you're too concerned about everything." It's a little game we play. Actually with me it's all going on, but subconsciously. My mind is very active and things are falling into place. The music, rehearsal time, plane reservations, dresses. It's all there. There's no detailed paper-work plan cut and dried, but it is taking shape anyway. The thought of living my life according to some careful plan worries me. That seems false to me. I thrive on the excitement of life as it happens. If I make a plan, there is always the feeling that the disappointment could be too great if things don't work as scheduled. Somehow I figure that life has been laid out for us. We have only to live it and enjoy it as we go along.

Point of View

Playing Atlanta, Georgia, in *Dolly* was a real kick for me. I'd gone there two Sundays before on promotion, and the town had just knocked me out, so I was really ready to return for the opening. On the promotion trip, I had gone to the Atlanta Braves ball field and had met, live, the Indian who dances every time they hit a home run. No one else in the cast had been there.

When we arrived at the airport, we got the royal treatment, unmatched anyplace else. My friend E.B., who was in the cast, was a little uncomfortable anyway. He had not been to the South before, and he was thinking, "Where is the Ku Klux Klan I've heard so much about?" All the stories he had ever heard about the South were still somewhere dormant in the back of his mind, despite the overwhelming hospitality.

At the theater, some things went wrong, and the cast was a little tense because I was having a particularly rough time with my fatigue—the heart problem had been building for quite a while. I was throwing so much nitroglycerin under my tongue that I could have blown up the theater if I'd wanted to. Naturally, the audience never knew about all the tension.

I did the finale in a lovely white dress. Suddenly, at the end of the finale, a figure vaulted over the rope that blocks the stairs to the stage. E.B., who had been looking the other way, turned just in time to catch a glimpse. He relates it thusly: "As this figure jumped over the ropes, all I could see was the white of that dress and somebody coming very fast. I closed my eyes, saying to myself, 'Oh my Lord, they've got our Pearlie Mae. First Martin Luther King, now Pearlie Mae.' I went out of my mind. When I opened my eyes again, you were doing 'Indian Love Call' with the Indian from the ball field, but I didn't know who he was. All I knew was that you were running around the ramp saying, 'Catch me.' For a fleeting second I thought, this is it, they've got her for sure. It is the end. She's dead and going to heaven."

E.B. hadn't completely recovered from his shock and his fears by closing night, a Sunday. Again the finale came and everyone was standing and cheering. E.B. tells it this way:

"She went down from the stage into the audience, like Moses leading the people of Galilee. The 'Red Sea' opened and let her in. Then it closed around her. She disappeared from sight. Then I knew, 'Oh Lordy, they've got her for sure now.' The theater was dark, and finally, after a very long time I saw that white dress and Pearlie Mae smiling, kissing, shaking hands with everyone. When she got close enough I said, 'Pearlie, get your shoes and let's get the hell out of here.' "

Apple Valley, California

Many men come here to die
They will tell you so in the check-out line
At the supermarket.
I was dead when I arrived,
And here to my distinct surprise
I have learned to live.
I sit on a rock
Looking at what is real—
Mountains, trees, birds, flowers,
Formations of clouds,

Sunrises, sunsets,
I feel love and warmth
In every one of God's possessions.
Indeed "What is man
That thou art mindful of him?"

Let Us Be Disturbed
Earthquake, Los Angeles, February 9, 1971

The earth is erupting, spinning around, pulling at the
seams, and in the wake of this we stand unaware and seemingly unafraid. Are we really both—unaware, yes; unafraid, no—but listening to that rumbling do we hear what
it's saying?

Run not from me but from yourselves. It's a terrifying
thought, isn't it, to think we have to move over for the forces
so much larger than us? Stop and think, if only for a moment. We have tried to move and create the forces, but it's
impossible. Something like them, yes, but never *them*. We
will not have to run or walk farther than ourselves—how
can we be afraid to walk away from that which can be taken
from us in one blow?

The earth quaked beneath us and we tried suddenly to
melt into one, but with the hardness of humanity we couldn't
quite blend into each other enough. It shook the very foundations. Fear was felt by all. It was truly like the end of the
world—at least that's what the feeling was, days, now
weeks, after, and the earth is still rumbling. So many sleep,
not hearing it, but it's not their fault, they can only hear
loud sounds.

If one could hear the beginning sound of an earthquake, the humming of the earth in that bass key, then the shake. . . . One asks which is worse—the beginning or the fantastic feeling while it moves or that after-shock inside yourself. I heard the sound, felt the fury, and listened to that terrible, frightening silence after and every tremor since. At first it was a strange kind of fear. I lay still. What was there to do while God was at work but just that? Was that an eternity we waited, Lord, for it to stop? Or was it just that minute man timed it to be by his earth machines?

All day I sat in the back yard. The sun was more brilliant than I've ever seen it and there was a large white circle around it. One couldn't look up at it, yet it was like the beginning of a new day. More rumbling came again and again.

The heavy ones always came in the black of night. Prayers must have been finally said by many. To pray what? "Dear God save us." Dear God (we could and probably should have prayed), we will start now to try to save ourselves—you did a long time ago. Liken us unto drowning men who, saved, pulled up on the beach, crawl back toward the ocean for water instead of going to the spring coming down from the mountain. Backward we go—comes the fear —forgetfulness— and back we go.

That day a thought came: "If men of all races, colors, and creeds at that moment could have lain down side by side, palms down, and held the earth still, they would have, and not looked at each other in hatred. But because we haven't done just that perhaps that's why the earth continues to shake."

I chose to think the least frightened of all were the children. Most of my strange fear came in the aftermath because man started into his busyness as soon as the earth stopped a moment. I don't mean helping-his-neighbor kind of thing; I mean general go-about-our-business attitude. For myself, I chose to sit calmly and wait, and in doing that I began to hear clearer what the earth was saying: "Be still." Move on to what I'm not sure yet, but in the stillness I feel deeply. While sleep comes to others I lie awake waiting for the "Big Boy." The creaking of the house, the spinning, the pulling apart at the very seams of the earth do not frighten me, they awe me. A child said something to me on the telephone—"God and you are such good buddies"—so I shall become even friendlier with my Buddy, not to use Him for only as long as the earth shakes, but because in the warmth of His friendship, He has always allowed me to sit under His wings, and there while He works I prefer to wait. When He says we move on, I move with my Friend, not as a burden, I hope, but because He asks me to go along as a friend to keep Him company.

Ours but To Do

I do not call myself a religious person, but other people call me one. I don't think that I've ever had an interview of more than five or six sentences without being asked, "You're a very religious person, aren't you?" Is it because I mention God? Is that enough? I don't think so. Some people mention God even as they spit in His face.

Several times I have been asked whether I am a pessimist or an optimist. My answer is always the same, "I am neither one, I am a realist." That's not the easiest thing in the world for people to be. Most folks don't like themselves well enough to be realists.

I am realist enough to know that I can't go on singing and performing forever, and that one day I will die. Now, don't get me wrong, I'm not anywhere near ready to give it up right now. But because I know that God writes the opening and closing dates on this engagement, it can't go on like this forever. I've got to do as much as I can right now, every minute.

What will happen to me when I can't sing and dance? Then I will do something else. I will do as much of it as I can, and I'll do it as well as I can. But I will do it. I have known all my life that when performing is gone, there will be something else in the world for me to do. I don't know exactly what it is, but it will bring me to sharing with a lot of people once again. I will keep doing, and I will be about my Father's business as best I can see it. Maybe I will share by studying and doing more writing. Maybe I will take an active interest in politics. Maybe I will run for President. Do you see what I'm saying? I cannot live without doing, even if the activity brings an end to me, kills me.

I have been close. With my illnesses, I have had people tell me to rest. Usually, these are the very people who tire me the most. I know what it means to be knocked completely out with fatigue. One day I guess I will get that big pain and a man will lean over me and say, "Pearl, you're going to die." I think maybe I would play house at that point. I would call everybody to my bedside and tell them, "I'm going to leave you soon. Don't worry about a thing. I'm not particular about leaving. Half the time I'm not sure what world I'm in anyway. All I know is that I *am* and I *live*."